Zombies

A HUNTER'S GUIDE

JOSEPH A. McCULLOUGH

First published in Great Britain in 2010 by Osprey Publishing,
Midland House, West Way, Botley, Oxford, OX2 0PH, UK
44-02 23rd Street, Suite 219, Long Island City, NY 11101, USA

E-mail: info@ospreypublishing.com

A CIP catalog record for this book is available from the British Library

ISBN 978 1 84908 395 9

Page layout by Myriam Bell Design, France
Index by David Worthington
Typeset in Goudy OldStyle, Chandler 42, Bank Gothic and Conduit ITC
Originated by PDQ Media, Bungay, UK
Printed in China through Bookbuilders

10 11 12 13 14 10 9 8 7 6 5 4 3 2 1

Osprey Publishing is supporting the Woodland Trust, the UK's leading woodland conservation charity, by funding the dedication of trees.

Dedication

I would like to thank my beautiful wife, Stephanie McCullough. It takes a wonderfully patient woman to support her husband in writing a book about walking, flesh-eating corpses.

Contents

Introduction

This book is dedicated to the men and women who have lost their lives defending our right to rest in peace.

In 2004, the United States Army granted me a rare privilege, a tour of the barracks and training grounds of the 34th Specialist Regiment at Fort Bragg in North Carolina. I visited the base on a quiet Sunday morning, when most of the soldiers were absent on leave. My guide was a young lieutenant, a two-year veteran of the unit. He

Artwork by Ana Mlinar

answered my questions with a laugh and a smile as he showed me around. Midway through the tour, we entered the motor pool where the "Nightmen" stored their Humvees and trucks. As I touched the armored sides of the vehicles, I realized that they were covered in scratches and claw marks.

Standing in that garage, my whole perception of the war against the undead changed. Up to that point, my study of zombies had always been a dry, if somewhat rare, academic pursuit. In dusty libraries it is easy to forget that zombies are creatures of rotting flesh and congealed blood. While I had battled for the pride of publication, the men and women of the 34th had stood on the frontlines, protecting us all from the worst nightmares of our childhood.

Since that day, I have devoted my time and energy to aiding the professional zombie hunters, through both academic research and potentially dangerous field work. I have traveled to several "hot zones," escorted by the containment teams of different nations, in an effort to obtain useful information. Despite owning an expensive 9mm pistol, I have never fired a shot at a zombie. I have run away from many.

I've come to realize that unlike those battered vehicles in the 34th motor pool, the scars of professional zombie hunters run deep, and the worst cannot be seen. The Zombie Wars have claimed many victims, and not all of them have died on a battlefield. While fiction and film have glorified zombies and zombie hunters, the truth is much grimmer.

I have written this book in an attempt to educate people about the true horrors of the zombie menace. The book opens with an individual analysis of each of the five main zombie varieties, while at the same time providing a short history of the zombie threat. It then covers some of the organizations that battle the undead and the weapons and tactics they employ.

It is my hope that readers will obtain a better understanding of the immense threat posed by the undead and gain a new respect for those who stand on the frontlines of the Zombie Wars.

Necromantic Zombies

The myths and legends of the ancient world are filled with stories of necromancers who could raise the dead and command them to do their bidding. These sorcerers often used their death magic to seize positions of power, becoming lords and kings and terrorizing their subjects with their undead armies. The great cities of Babylon and Nineveh particularly served as capitals of the necromantic arts, and from these centers the knowledge spread to the farthest corners of Europe and Asia. But in the early centuries after Christ, as his new religion began to take root in the Roman Empire, the art of necromancy fell into decline. The Christian faith viewed necromancy as the most vile and heinous of the ungodly magics. The early popes worked tirelessly to destroy all necromantic knowledge and to hunt down its practitioners. Still, necromancy survived. It is mentioned by Gildas in the dark days of Britain and in the accounts of numerous crusading knights. However, it was in the wilds of western China and the mountains of the Himalayas that the knowledge found safe haven and slowly started to filter back into Europe.

While Europe remained unified under one church, it remained relatively safe from the terrors of necromancy. True, isolated incidents that challenged the champions of chivalry were not uncommon, but gone were the vast hordes of shambling dead that had formed the armies of many an ancient tyrant. The necromancers of the European Middle Ages proved weak magicians, only able to command a few reanimated zombies or skeletons. Unfortunately, a major revival came with the dawn of the modern world.

In the sixteenth century, Christian unity shattered, first with Martin Luther and then with countless successors. In this time of chaos and confusion, the dark arts of necromancy crept back into Europe, thriving amidst a new time of bloodshed. Still, it was not until the vast slaughter of the Thirty Years' War that necromancers once again attempted to employ their death magic on a vast scale. Even a casual reader of the history of this time is likely to stumble across a reference or two. Perhaps the most common, and certainly the most terrifying, are the "sky battles." Found in the manuscripts of both commoners and lords, sky battles often occurred on a battlefield a day or two after the armies had moved on. Different accounts paint wildly different pictures, but all agree that the dead rose up once again and renewed their battle. A few people mention the living generals in these battles, but no one seems to know fully what they meant. It is only now, with 400 years of hindsight that we can understand these sky battles as the first steps in a new age of necromancy. Clearly some of the ancient knowledge had been lost. The new necromancers could raise up armies, but they could not yet control them. The fractured state of Europe proved the perfect testing ground to run their experiments, a land covered in corpses and lacking central authority.

Artwork by Charlie Adlard from *The Walking Dead*

Artwork by Eren Arik

From the darkness of the Thirty Years' War, it is easy to follow the progression of this new necromancy. The English Civil War saw the first controlled use of a zombie army in Europe since before Christ.[1] Soon thereafter it spread to the New World and established a permanent foothold. Napoleon, to his credit, seems to have understood the dangers of necromancy and for a while managed to nearly push it back out of Europe. Unfortunately, many of his enemies fled to Russia, and during Napoleon's invasion and subsequent retreat from Moscow, they exacted a terrible revenge. To this day it is unknown how many Frenchmen or their allies were killed by the dead hands of one of their own army.

With the allied victory at Waterloo, Europe settled into a period of outward expansion, and thus unwittingly spread necromancy to all corners of the globe. In America, the necromancers for the first time showed a sense of patriotism and waged their own war under the cover of their Civil War. While the number of necromantic incidents in this conflict are far too numerous to mention, it is perhaps worth noting that the "Second Battle of Gettysburg" remains the single most recorded and studied clash of necromantic forces in history.

The twentieth century actually witnessed a reversal of fortune for students of necromancy. Perhaps the death wizards had overplayed their hand in the Civil War, for governments around the world began to recognize the threat and the first government-backed zombie-hunter teams were formed. Also, numerous private and religious organizations joined in the fight. By World War I, the necromancers were on the run, and they played only a limited role in the Great War. In World War II, their services were shunned by the Allies, and many took refuge in the welcoming arms of Nazi Germany (see Chapter 3).

Since World War II, necromancy has remained a constant low-level threat the world over. Free governments have worked together to fight against these dark wizards, and Communism also proved a bitter opponent of magic in all its forms. Today it is estimated that there are between 200 and 1,000 practicing necromancers in the world, with Africa having a greater number than anywhere else. For many reasons discussed below, necromantic zombies do not pose the same level of threat as the newer varieties, but they are still a dangerous force that has been driven to the brink of extinction before only to find new life in a new era.

---

1 Generally called "The March on Salisbury," a horde of several hundred zombies was eventually hunted down and exterminated by a group of royalist cavalry.

CENTERS FOR NECROMANTIC AND ANIMATE NECROLOGY STUDIES

Miskatonic University, Arkham, Massachusetts
Despite its sinister reputation as "Suicide University," Miskatonic remains the world's foremost place of study for alternate theology, prehistoric philosophy, and animate necrology. Its 10,000 volumes on animate necrology comprise the single greatest collection in the world and helped greatly in the production of this work. While access to the library has become more restricted in recent years, it is still possible for those who are working in the field to gain passes without too much trouble.

The University of North Carolina, Chapel Hill
Under the leadership of Special Collections Administrator Douglas Hudson, the University of North Carolina at Chapel Hill (UNC) has quietly accumulated one of the most impressive collections of necromantic texts in the western hemisphere. Among the documents that can be found in the third subbasement of Davis Library are a copy of *De Vermis Mysteriis*, the Pnokotic Manuscripts, and several leafs of an original Arabic version of the *Necronomicon*. Thankfully, the university has realized both the value and danger of this collection and has greatly increased the security staff for its library system. Passes to see the collection are incredibly difficult to obtain, and even those with a legitimate need should expect to wait at least two years before gaining admittance.

The Vatican Archive, Vatican City
Most of what is contained in the Vatican's legendary *Corpus Mortuambulanticum* is pure conjecture, but there are few who doubt it to be the single greatest repository of necromantic knowledge in the world. Virtually inaccessible and guarded by some of the world's best soldiers, it remains the private domain of the Catholic Church, the Swiss Guard, and the Vatican Containment Soldiers, "The Bringers of Peace." Constant demands by a few individuals in the animate necrology community to open up the archives have fallen on deaf ears. In point of fact, there are many, this author included, who believe the world is a safer place if those archives remain closed.

The Bodleian Library, Oxford
The world-famous Bodleian Library has made no special effort to acquire or catalog material relating to the undead, but nevertheless, it contains the most extensive and varied selection of works pertaining to revenants available. Many, if not most, of these accounts live only in manuscript form, and there are probably dozens that remain undiscovered along the endless miles of dusty shelves. The Bodleian is not open to the general public, but passes are not hard to obtain. Please note that because many of the manuscripts remain uncataloged, it is important to have a clear idea of the manuscript you need before you enter the library.

CREATION

Like all forms of magic, necromancy is an art, not a science. It has few hard and fast rules, and it is often the variation and individual flair that gives it strength. Even if I were so inclined, it would not be possible to give the basics of even a single spell to reanimate the dead in the space I have available. The famous grimoires, the great treasures of necromancy, are all vast tomes running for thousands of pages, often only covering a few spells. But even these should be seen as only rough guides and not zombie cookbooks. Their danger lies in their power of suggestion, their hints of greater and greater power. Most necromantic knowledge is passed directly from wizard to wizard or garnered through individual research.

With all of that in mind, it is possible to present some of the more common elements of magical zombie creation in order that the process can be better understood and countered. Long ago, there may have been necromancers who could raise the dead with no more than a few words and a wave of the hand, but if so, those days are long gone. Even for today's most powerful sorcerers, reanimation is a slow, messy process requiring a van-load of materials. First and foremost, the process requires a "cauldron." Anything that can hold liquid can serve as a cauldron, but the nature of the vessel will have subtle influences on the zombies created, and metal is still the preferred cauldron material. Also, it is best if the cauldron is big enough to hold a human body. Many bargain-basement necromancers have taken to using oil drums, which seems to produce a slightly more bad-tempered zombie.

Into the cauldron goes a classic witch's brew. The list of possible ingredients is never-ending, and each can have subtle effects on the zombie produced. However, one component that is central to all undead concoctions is fresh blood, the fresher the better. It might be possible to use animal blood, but considering the other main component is a corpse, human blood is the norm. All of the ingredients are added in a precise order over a number of days, usually accompanied by incantations and/or ritualized dancing. The entire process can take anywhere from three days to three months, and more often than not, it fails.

It is perhaps this high rate of failure that has saved us all from becoming the slaves (or ingredients) of the necromancers. Professor Katherine de Rowe of Oxford University, in her ground-breaking paper *The Spread of Death Magic*,[2] stated that "One highly skilled necromancer is more dangerous than one hundred novices...," and this is mainly due to their success rate in creating the undead. She also goes on to point out that nearly 80 percent of novice necromancers are killed in their first year of dabbling in the dark arts, although this statistic is highly debated.

In the instances where the sorcery succeeds and a viable brew is concocted, the necromancer proceeds to either dunk a corpse into the cauldron or pour the contents onto the ground where a corpse is buried. This is generally accompanied by more incantations. Several necromantic texts state that dunking is preferable to pouring, but no official studies have ever been conducted. It takes a newly created zombie only minutes to wake up, although if it has to claw its way out of a casket or up out of the ground, it may take a while before it appears.

Although there is no exact liquid-to-zombie ratio, the bigger the cauldron the more zombies it can produce. It is also possible to store the liquid in sealed containers for later use. With stored brew, a necromancer can quickly create zombies; however, zombies created in this fashion are generally weaker than those created from fresh stock.

IDENTIFICATION AND THREAT

Even at a great distance, the undead nature of a necromantic zombie is pretty obvious, although distinguishing it from other types of horde zombie might prove difficult.[3] Like their atomic cousins, necromantic zombies are slow, shambling creatures. Their gait appears unnatural and unbalanced, often made worse by missing or broken limbs. An overwhelming stench of death and decay accompanies these zombies. In the case of

[2] *The Journal of Animate Necrology*, Miskatonic University Press, Vol. 39 No. 2

[3] The term "horde zombie" is sometimes used to group necromantic, atomic, and viral zombies together as these three types share a similar "herd mentality" and often form together in large groups.

large hordes, this smell has been known to hit living beings with an almost physical force that can cause nausea, vomiting, and even fainting. Unlike other zombie types, necromantic zombies never speak, moan, or produce any other sound with their throats. Long-time zombie hunters who have faced multiple types of undead often claim that this silence is actually more terrifying than the horrific moans of atomic zombies.

In appearance, there is one significant difference between zombies raised by magic and those created by other means. Chemical and viral zombification only affects the recently deceased, whereas magic can reanimate a corpse hundreds, even thousands of years old. For most of its short history, the science of animate necrology classified walking skeletons as a unique family of undead; however, current thought places them as a subtype of the necromantic zombie. In fact, the only major difference between skeletons and other zombies is that the skeletons are a bit more fragile but also slightly quicker. (Apparently all that flesh was just slowing them down.) In a couple of instances, necromancers have also used zombification to reanimate an ancient mummy, but these too are just a peculiar brand of zombie and not a true living mummy.

Because of their potential age, necromantic zombies often spawn in an advanced state of decomposition, and it is not uncommon for a shambler to leave a trail of rotting flesh and small body parts. More often than not, these zombies have empty eye sockets, exposed bones, dangling or trailing innards, and missing jawbones. They are almost always accompanied by black clouds of carrion crows or other flesh-eating fowl.

Should a zombie hunter overcome the stench and terror of a horde of magically fueled corpses, another nasty surprise awaits. Necromantic zombies carry guns. Or, to be more accurate, necromantic zombies are capable of using weapons. In most cases these will be simple bludgeoning or cutting weapons, the rusty knife being the most ubiquitous. However, zombies animated from professional soldiers or hunters accustomed to carrying firearms during life will continue to do so in death. True, their aim tends to be wild, but even zombies occasionally get in a lucky shot. Thankfully, these zombies are incapable of most other feats of manual dexterity, including reloading. It is up to the necromancer or his living servants to arm his zombies before he sends them on campaign.

In hand-to-hand combat, necromantic zombies are the weakest variety of zombie. While strength varies considerably based on the skill of the necromancer, few of these zombies could match the strength of a full-grown man, and some are considerably weaker. One-on-one, most people should be able to defeat, or at least escape from, a necromantic zombie. Unfortunately, they are rarely encountered individually.

The goal of most necromancers is to build a vast army of zombie warriors for the purpose of conquest, but without a necromancer to guide them, magically created zombies have no will or intelligence of their own. Without specific instructions they will stand stock-still, unresponsive to any movement or threat. That does not mean a necromancer must be physically present to guide them. Zombies can be commanded to guard specific items or locations, with orders to kill intruders or would-be thieves. They can also be sent out to attack specific places or people or even to recover objects. They cannot, however, perform any action requiring a particular skill set. In fact, doorknob usage appears to be beyond their comprehension, although breaking down a door through weight of numbers does not.

ELIMINATION AND PREVENTION

Ask any professional zombie killer which variety of zombie he least wants to face, and the answer will invariably be necromantic. This is not because they are particularly tough or dangerous, but because their elimination is incredibly messy. Unlike revenants or other horde zombies, necromantic zombies possess no single weakness. Since many lack any kind of brain, and some even lack heads, hunters cannot rely on the classic head shot or decapitation. Instead, the only way to kill a necromantic zombie is to bash it to pieces.[4] There really is no scientific way to state this. These zombies are bound together by magic, and it is only through mangling and dismembering the corpse that the spell can be physically broken. Exactly how much damage a zombie can take depends on the skill of the necromancer who created it in the first place. If a zombie does possess a head, shattering the skull will normally do the trick. Otherwise, it is probably best to go for the spinal column. More often than not, breaking the zombie in two will also break the spell that animates it. If not, it will at least severely slow it down.

While machetes, *katanas*, and aluminum baseball bats are probably the ideal necromantic zombie killers and one should certainly be carried as backup, it is always best to take zombies out at a distance. The key for eliminating necromantic zombies with gunfire is caliber. While a .22 might be used effectively for sniping the brains out of other horde zombies, its lack of punch makes it mostly useless against magically powered corpses. If you want to kill these zombies, you need something that can blow off big chunks. At a minimum, hunters will want .45s, which is why so many modern hunters carry a Colt 1911 as their sidearm. However, the king of zombie killers remains the shotgun. Armed with either slugs or shot, at close range, a shotgun blast to the chest or head will generally take a zombie down.

The best solution to a necromantic zombie incursion or threat, and one that is unique to this variety, is killing the necromancer. Although not an easy task, finding and eliminating the necromancer that created the zombies will break the spell, and the corpses will immediately deanimate, crumpling into a pile of flesh and bones.

Artwork by Gracjana Zielinska

There are some people out there, even a few within the animate necrology community, who argue the value of "white magic." There is certainly compelling evidence that some forms of magic can be used to effectively combat the undead.

4 Linguistics is still searching for words to replace "kill" and "fatal" in discussions of the undead. Since none have yet been found, I will continue to use them.

LICHES

Put simply, a liche is an undead necromancer, and thankfully, they are incredibly rare. To become a liche, a death wizard commits a form of magical suicide in which the body is killed, but the soul is bound to the reanimated corpse. Whether a liche is a zombie remains a topic of academic debate, but at a minimum they should be considered an extremely dangerous form of magical zombie master. In appearance they resemble their zombie servants, with frail bodies withered by their own magic; however, that is where the similarities end. Liches possess all of the knowledge, skills, and abilities they possessed in life, including their magical abilities. They think, reason, and speak. They also seem to maintain whatever dexterity they had in life.

Since liches remain so rare, there is little that can be said about them with certainty. Liches have no known weakness. Massive amounts of physical damage may be able to destroy the magical bonds that hold them together, but this has never been put to the test. Incineration is probably the best bet. If there are currently any liches in the world, they have remained hidden. Then again, when you are already dead, time is on your side.

Artwork by Geneviève Morge

However – and I want to state this as clearly as possible – "white magic" and "death magic" are vague and nearly meaningless terms. At best, they are two sides of the same coin. At worst, "white magic" is just a slightly cleaner form of necromancy. Both are at odds with the natural world. While the temptation to fight fire with fire remains great, it is always better to trust your 12-gauge than some ancient incantation.

Of course, where necromantic zombies are concerned, the best solution is prevention, as it is easy to put the deceased beyond the clutches of even the most powerful death wizard. A corpse cannot be reanimated if it has been buried or interred with the proper rites and rituals of a monotheistic religion. Some people have argued that this is proof of the power of white magic, but more likely it is a flaw or weakness in the spells of necromancy. Since necromancy developed in societies where monotheism was rare, or nonexistent, it seems the early wizards never factored the idea into their magic. Either way, it works. Christian, Jewish, or Muslim makes no difference; the rites of each will stop necromancers cold. This also helps explain why necromancers are most prevalent during great wars, when thousands of corpses are left strewn across the earth, having never received their final rites.

Voodoo Zombies

When the rise of Christianity drove the necromancers out of Europe, one group disappeared into the wilds of West Africa. Over the centuries, they wormed their way into positions of power and incorporated aspects of their black magic, including the creation of zombies, into the local religions. Records from this time are almost nonexistent, and what little information we have comes from ancient folklore. However, this strain of necromancy slowly re-emerged with the rise of the slave trade in the sixteenth and seventeenth centuries. As the European slavers transplanted thousands of native Africans, including many witch doctors, to the islands of the Caribbean, the African religions slowly mixed with Roman Catholicism to create the culture of voodoo. And with this culture came a new variety of zombie.

US Marines stationed in Haiti in the early twentieth century.

Technically, voodoo zombies are a subclassification of necromantic zombies, but since they have been studied in isolation for so long, and because their magical reanimation contains so many unique elements, most animate necrologists continue to view them as a separate category. In fact, the most important contributions to the study of voodoo zombies have been made by anthropologists, most of whom are either unaware or unconcerned with the greater threat of the undead.

A rare photograph of a voodoo zombie.

Voodoo took strongest root in the nation of Haiti, and it is there that a majority of voodoo zombies are found. Even so, voodoo is practiced by over sixty million people worldwide, including strong concentrations in parts of North, South, and Central America as well as the other islands of the Caribbean. In fact, voodoo had one of its strongest followings among the Creole people of Louisiana, and it is from their language that the word "zombie" originates. After the American Civil War, many of the Creole practitioners of voodoo were rounded up in the general pursuit of necromancers, and today the darker practices of voodoo only survive in America in the back streets of New Orleans and the most isolated parts of the Louisiana bayou.

After successfully tackling the zombie problem at home, the United States attempted to strike against the heart of voodoo. After the lynching of Haitian President Jean Vibrun Guillaume Sam in 1915, the US Marines led an invasion of Haiti, ostensibly to restore order. Over the next twenty years, the Marines engaged in a systematic attempt to stamp out voodoo across the island.

Despite America's clandestine war against necromancy and voodoo, most of the citizens of the Western world remained blissfully ignorant of the undead threat. This began to change in 1932 with the publication of *The Magic Island* by William B. Seabrook. While many modern ethnologists have labeled the book "sensationalist trash," Seabrook's account of his travels through Haiti includes many details about voodoo, including an encounter with a zombie. The book caught the public imagination, especially the zombie incident, and soon the idea spread to Hollywood. In 1932, *The White Zombie*, starring Béla Lugosi, hit theaters across the United States and launched a new genre of horror film that continues to cloud and confuse the true study of zombies to this day.

The United States withdrew its forces from Haiti in 1934. Although the Marines had made a thorough effort to eradicate voodoo, it survived and slowly rebuilt. In 1950, François "Papa Doc" Duvalier came to power in Haiti and fostered the regrowth of voodoo. For twenty years, Duvalier ruled the country through a fear partially inspired by the black magic of voodoo. Some claim that he created his own small army of zombie soldiers, though this has never been confirmed.

Political upheaval eventually forced Papa Doc's son and heir to flee the country, and thus ended the governmental support of voodoo. The practice remains strong, however, and America continues to send agents to the island to monitor the situation.

WADE DAVIS

The foremost researcher into Haitian voodoo zombies, Wade Davis came to prominence in 1985 after the publication of his book, *The Serpent and the Rainbow*. In its pages, Davis first revealed the importance of zombie powder in the creation process. Davis even managed to obtain samples of this powder, which revealed the presence of tetrodotoxin. In response to criticism, Davis followed up his first book with a second, *Passage of Darkness: The Ethnobiology of the Haitian Zombie*, in which he presents further evidence. While it remains unclear whether Wade Davis ever saw a true necromantic voodoo zombie or just a fake zombie produced by diluted zombie powder, his works have brought valuable attention to the Haitian zombie problem.

CREATION

The strain of necromancy that lives within voodoo has a distinct flavor that sets it apart from the death magic of Europe and Asia. The wielders of this magic are called bokors,[5] and even within their own culture are usually viewed as pariahs. While these bokors deal in all kinds of black magic, including fetishes and charms, they are most feared for their ability to create zombies. Unlike Western necromantic zombie creation that only deals with corpses, the creation of a voodoo zombie involves capturing a person's soul.

Artwork by Michael Maier

Among ghost hunters and others who study the ethereal undead, it is a well-established fact that an individual's soul lingers near its body for a least a day or two after death, before continuing on to its second existence. During this period of lingering, souls are at their most vulnerable to necromancy. Using their dark arts, bokors can imprison souls in a sealed jar or trap them inside a fetish. These imprisoned souls are known as *zombi astral* and are forced to do the bidding of their captor. A *zombi astral* can be released by shattering the jar or fetish holding it.[6]

Once a bokor has imprisoned a soul, he can command the corresponding body to rise up from death, using a substance known as zombie powder. This powder is basically a solid form of the brew used by other necromancers, though it contains several unique elements such as tetrodotoxin, an extremely powerful poison found in some puffer fish and octopi.

---

[5] "Bokor" can have different meanings depending on where it is used. I am using it only in its most common definition.

[6] Despite their name, *zombi astral* are an ethereal form of undead, and thus beyond the scope of this investigation.

Bokors sprinkle the powder into the mouth of a corpse while taunting it with its own captured soul. After rising, the zombie remains under the command of whoever controls the vessel in which its soul is imprisoned.

It is worth noting that many bokors use zombie powder as a poison, slipped into food. There is no cure for this poison, and death normally occurs within four to six hours. Afterward, a bokor can quickly trap the soul and raise the zombie without a further application of powder.

Because voodoo zombies require the trapping of the soul, it is only possible to create them from the newly deceased.

IDENTIFICATION AND THREAT

Voodoo zombies are the least immediately recognizable form of zombie. From a distance, they appear to be normal human beings, though perhaps a bit slow and lethargic. Up close, however, it is a different story. Voodoo zombies have empty, soulless eyes, slack-jawed expressions, and very slow movements. They do occasionally speak, responding to direct questions in a nasal voice devoid of emotion. A few bokors sew the mouths of their zombies shut, to prevent them from eating salt. Due to a peculiarity of voodoo necromancy, the ingesting of salt causes a voodoo zombie to go wild, attacking the bokor that created it.

Like all forms of necromantic zombie, voodoo zombies are capable of using weapons and even tools. In fact, it is probably more common for this variety of zombie to be used for manual labor than as a weapon. When they are armed, most zombies carry the traditional Haitian machete, a weapon they wield with lifeless indifference. Otherwise, they will attack with their hands, displaying normal human strength.

In comparison to other forms of zombie, voodoo zombies offer little threat to mankind as a whole. The process of creating zombie powder is long, difficult, and expensive, and its use is limited to the newly deceased. Thus bokors are unlikely to assemble the large armies of other necromancers. On the other hand, the threat to the individual of being raised as a zombie is incalculable. With the possible exception of revenants, all other forms of zombie are the product of corpses whose souls have departed this earth. Voodoo zombism is the ultimate threat, the idea of slavery and imprisonment even after death. It is perhaps the greatest evil that necromancy has to offer and the main reason that the US government and other zombie-hunting agencies have worked so hard to stamp out the black magic of voodoo.

François "Papa Doc" Duvalier, President of Haiti from 1957 until his death in 1971.

Getty Images

PSEUDO-VOODOO ZOMBIES

Research into voodoo zombies has often been confused by the presence of "fake zombies" or "living zombies." Haiti remains a poorly policed state, and in many areas local gang bosses use the threat of zombification to terrify the populace. But these greedy and dangerous individuals rarely agree to pay for the services of a bokor, even if one can be found. Instead, these men sometimes buy a diluted form of zombie powder, which they use to poison those who attempt to defy them. While not poisonous enough to kill, the powder causes a deep paralysis. The gang then buries their victim in a mock funeral and leaves them trapped underground for half a day. The victim, still suffering from the poison and partial asphyxiation, is then dug up and beaten. The effect of this horrendous treatment can often break the spirit of an individual and reduce him to a highly suggestible, half-comatose state that resembles zombification in many ways.

These fake zombies have led to many cases of mistaken identity, and have made both bokors and voodoo zombies appear to be much more common than is actually the case. While the Haitian government has outlawed the use of drugs as a means of threat or intimidation, this does little to stop the practice. Fake zombies have also led to the creation of several "zombie rehabilitation centers," a concept that would be laughable in the case of true zombies.

ELIMINATION AND PREVENTION

The most fragile of all zombie types, voodoo zombies can be eliminated by either destroying the brain or through large amounts of damage to the body. A single shotgun blast or several shots from an assault rifle usually takes them down. Unlike other necromantic zombie types, killing a bokor does not automatically destroy his zombies, but the zombies will deanimate the second that their *zombi astral* is set free.

Because of their long association with the black magic of voodoo, the inhabitants of Haiti have invented many ways of preventing a loved one from becoming a zombie. Since cremation is generally out of the question, many families elect to rekill a corpse by destroying the brain or cutting the throat. Some even go so far as to sew the mouths shut to make the application of zombie powder more difficult. The most common form of prevention is for the family to stand guard over the body or grave for two days after death, ensuring that the soul safely passes on to the next world.

Bokor with voodoo zombie

While voodoo zombies are rarely employed as weapons, most bokors select a couple of their smartest and toughest creations to act as bodyguards, using them to intimidate their foes and to provide cover if a quick getaway proves necessary. Note the zombie with the sewn mouth. This may have been done by the family of the deceased individual to try to protect against zombification, or just as likely, by the necromancer himself to try to guard against the dangers of salt.

Nazi Zombies

Hidden beneath the British World War II codebreaking center at Bletchley Park is a vast basement, officially called "The Cloak Room." All access points to the rooms were sealed in 1947, and since then no one, government or civilian, has set eyes on the place. According to the records, the Cloak Room served as an intelligence gathering center, but those records are exceedingly vague as to what information was collected. It is only in recent years, as the generation that worked in those rooms has begun to pass on, that a few whispered voices have spoken about the place as the location of Supreme Allied Command: Shadow Theater (SAC:ST). It was from these rooms that American General E. L. Whately organized a war within a war and led the battle against the Nazi Occult Division. While credit and honor is justly given to the Allied soldiers who fought against the Nazi war machine, the men and women who worked for SAC:ST should also be remembered. If not for their tireless efforts and great sacrifices, Allied victory might have proved impossible and the earth consumed by an endless tide of Nazi undead.

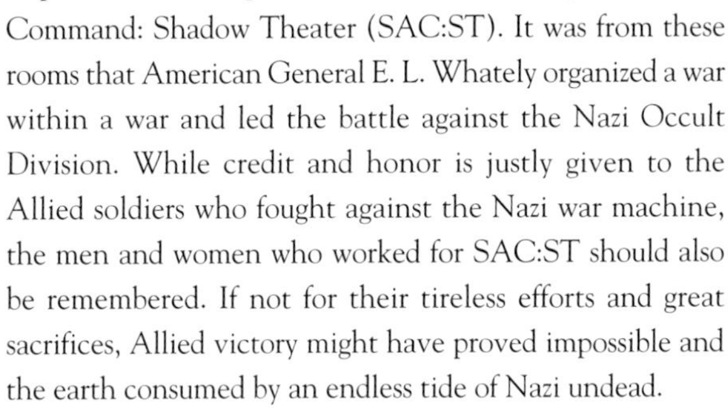

Artwork by James J. Frazier

The story of the Nazi undead program begins in 1917 when a wounded German World War I veteran named Walter Nauhaus founded the Society of Thule.[7] Based in Munich, the secret order devoted itself to the pursuit of necromantic knowledge. With the end of the Great War, the society expanded, adding new members from across Germany, including Adolf Hitler. Through subtle manipulations, Hitler and his supporters shifted the attention of most of the group away from occult rituals toward the idea of Aryan supremacy and melded the society with the German Workers' Party.

[7] Thule was one of the great empires of prehistory. At its peak it contained all of Scandinavia and most of northern Germany. While all of the names of its rulers have been lost, there is an indication that it had only one great emperor, a liche who ruled for over 400 years.

Bundesarchiv

The Nazi expedition to Tibet.

However, with the dissolution of the Society of Thule, Hitler founded a new group called "The Brotherhood of Death," which included all of the foremost occultists from the old society. As Hitler rose to power in Germany, the Brotherhood rose with him. Word leaked across the globe that necromancers everywhere would be safe and welcomed by the Nazis. By the mid-1930s, it is estimated that between thirty and forty practicing necromancers had joined the Nazi ranks, and at least three times that number of acolytes were in training.

Thankfully, European necromancy was still suffering from the governmental offensives since the American Civil War. Huge amounts of knowledge had been lost. While a few sightings of early Nazi zombie experiments occurred in the 1930s, they were few and far between. The senior members of the Brotherhood knew they would have to look beyond the borders of Europe to regain this knowledge, and they pressed Hitler to organize an expedition to the Himalayas. Hitler, now busy with other matters, passed the request along to Heinrich Himmler, who in turn found his man in the SS officer, Ernst Schäfer. The young and popular Schäfer had already participated in two expeditions into Tibet, and he wanted to lead his own. A student of anthropology, Schäfer had no interest in necromancy and originally refused to take any such wizards on his team. However, after the tragic death of his wife in a hunting accident, Schäfer had a change of heart and allowed several members of the Brotherhood to accompany the mission.

The expedition proved a tremendous success, for Nazi propaganda, for European anthropology, and for the necromancers of The Brotherhood of Death. There are no records of exactly what knowledge the Brotherhood obtained, but the expedition marked a turning point in their efforts. From 1939 onward, the Nazi undead program slowly gained strength and confidence. There are at least two recorded incidents of

The Crusader forces attacking Antioch, where they discovered the Spear of Longinus.

Polish villages being attacked by zombified Polish soldiers. In 1940, the Nazis unleashed a unit of armed and uniformed zombies called the *Todesritter* (or "Death Knights") during their invasion of Denmark.

While the *Todesritter* proved effective shock units, even the dozens of necromancers employed by the Nazis could not make a material difference in a war that would eventually involve millions. Hitler demanded a weapon that could sweep his enemies aside, especially the Russians. The Brotherhood, using the knowledge acquired in Tibet, realized the only way to produce such an army would be to overcome the monotheistic burial limitation, and the only hope of that lay in finding some of the ancient artifacts of the great religions. Thus the Nazis launched Operation *Eklipse*.

While *Eklipse* saw many successes and failures, three missions stood far above the rest in importance. The first was the search for the Ark of the Covenant. The Nazis did briefly obtain the Ark, however American agents managed to recapture it before it could do any damage.[8] The second was the search for *Zulfiqar*, the legendary sword of Muhammad, which ended in disaster when an entire German division fell prey to an ancient curse. The last was the mission to capture the Spear of Destiny, better known to Western readers as the Spear of Longinus – the holy lance that pierced the side of Jesus Christ as he hung on the cross. In 1941 a group of *Fallschirmjäger* (German paratroopers) recovered the lance from its hiding place in Antioch, and removed it back to Germany. With this lance, the necromancers of the Brotherhood believed that they could raise up the millions upon millions of dead who had been buried with Christian rites.

We will likely never know the full story of the grim battle waged by the forces of the SAC:ST to recapture the spear, nor the names of the men and women who died ensuring it could never be used. All we really know is that for the next three years the spear was moved all over Germany, but everywhere the Nazis took it, Allied agents were waiting to pounce. The toll of these suicide missions must have stretched the SAC:ST to the limit, but in the end, it was enough. Hounded at every turn, the Brotherhood never had a chance to make use of the spear or its potential power. In 1945, elements of Patton's armored forces recovered the spear, which was shipped back to the United States. Its current whereabouts are unknown.

Without the Spear of Longinus, the necromancers never played a decisive role in World War II. That said, they still exacted a terrible price on the Allies. On the Eastern Front it is estimated that the Nazis created nearly a million zombies. Most of

[8] The US government has worked hard to keep all information pertaining to the Ark a secret. There is at least one famous account of the Nazi capture of the Ark that only got past the censors because it changed all of the names of those involved, and even moved the date to several years before the war.

Previous page: Nazi zombies

The largest concentration of Nazi zombie forces was deployed during the Kursk offensive in 1943. While primarily remembered as a tank battle, the Germans began their attack by unleashing several divisions of *Todesritter* against the Russian defenses. While these zombies created havoc in the first tier of the Russian fortifications, they soon became isolated and proved easy prey for a Russian armored counterattack. Casualties for these battles are nearly impossible to calculate as it is difficult to determine which soldiers were dead before the battle started.

these were flung at the Russians during the German retreat to Berlin. At first, the *Todesritter* proved extremely effective against the conscripted and poorly motivated Russian troops. However, even for the dead, the laws of warfare still applied. The Nazi zombie hordes could never achieve complete victory without armored support, armor the Nazis just didn't possess by that phase of the war. Despite the damage they inflicted, most of the *Todesritter* ended up ground beneath the treads of T-34 tanks.

In the aftermath of the war, members of the Brotherhood were hunted down and executed. Since the exact composition of the group remains unknown, it is impossible to say whether or not they were all captured, but it seems clear that a majority were dead by 1947.

The Nazi zombie program is the closest the earth has come to the dark days of prehistory, when necromantic zombies stalked the earth in vast armies. While the Russians did prove that modern technology has lessened this threat, it should not be ignored. The possibility that one of the ancient artifacts could be recovered and break the bonds of monotheism is a dark and sobering thought. Also, the idea of state-sponsored necromancy should continue to be seen as one of the most dangerous forms of weapons development on the planet.

Revenants

"It would not be easy to believe that the corpses of the dead should sally from their graves, and should wander about to the terror or destruction of the living ... did not frequent examples, occurring in our own times, suffice to establish this fact."
William of Newburgh, *Historia rerum Anglicarum*

Revenants are one of the first classifications of zombie that can be positively identified in historical sources. The Vikings called them *draug* or *draugr* and often included them in their semimythical sagas. However, it is with the later English medieval writers William of Newburgh and Walter Map that the first documented revenant attacks can be found. For the undead that stalk these tales clearly show the individuality, the malignant intelligence, and most importantly, the overwhelming sense of purpose that define these zombies.

Thankfully, due to their relative rarity and their individual nature, revenants do not offer the same level of threat to mankind posed by their more common cousins. That said, individually, revenants are far and away the most dangerous type of zombie, and their elimination should be left in the hands of trained professionals.

Artwork by Grzegorz Krysiński

CREATION

Unlike every other form of zombie, revenants are not created through any identifiable external source. They are not magical, chemical, or viral, nor are they self-replicating. People who come into contact with a revenant have no

Revenants

Best method of permanent elimination: incineration

chance of being infected or becoming undead (although "dead" is a likely outcome). Instead, the force that reanimates a revenant seems to come completely from within the deceased individual.[9] This force, which is normally termed "drive" or "purpose," is most often a single strong emotion or desire, the most common of which are anger and revenge.

While the creation process is not fully understood, the revenants' drive makes them similar in nature to several forms of ethereal undead such as ghosts and wraiths, and like those spirits, revenants are often said to "haunt" an individual or location. This comparison should not be carried too far, however, because unlike ghosts, revenants are in no way bound to a specific local. Instead, their drive tends to lead them to specific places. In the case of revenge, revenants will hunt down their target, following wherever that target goes. Where the drive is a more general anger, revenants tend to stay in one location, their graveyard, their home, or the scene of a major life event.

Less commonly, some revenants return from the dead in quest of a specific object. Termed "Rose Bud Syndrome" after the 1951 "Hearst Incident," these zombies are no less deadly than ones motivated by anger or revenge, and will literally tear people in half if they come between them and their desire. There have been several cases where the object of a revenant's drive has been a specific person, but do not be fooled into thinking that "love" ever plays a part in the makeup of any zombie. There has been no evidence of love or any other "good" emotion ever leading to the creation of a revenant.

Artwork by Jamie Luning

IDENTIFICATION AND THREAT

In many ways, revenants do not fit the modern conception of the zombie, and for this reason they are often misidentified. At a distance, revenants are difficult to distinguish from the living. Although their movements are somewhat slow and mechanical, they are not outside human norms and are a far cry from shuffling gait of most

[9] Many leading animate necrologists still argue that there is a metaphysical element to the process. However, discussions of Satan or other embodiments of evil are beyond this investigation.

RE-KILLING BILLY THE KID

Undoubtedly the most famous revenant of modern times was William Bonney, better known by his alias, Billy the Kid. Born around the beginning of the American Civil War, Billy rose to prominence during the "Lincoln County War," a bitter struggle between rival ranchers in New Mexico in 1877. During the fighting, Billy proved himself a remorseless killer, and in the years that followed, he traveled around the West working as a hired gun and gambler and leaving a trail of bodies in his wake. Finally, in 1881, a sheriff named Pat Garrett shot Billy dead with a bullet to the brain, but the story doesn't end there.

A great mystery surrounds the last minutes of Billy the Kid's life. For one, some claim that Pat Garrett and Billy were old friends, and, if true, it certainly helps explain what happened next. Billy was buried at Fort Sumner in New Mexico, but two weeks later a soldier from the Fort discovered a hole in Billy's grave. Billy's body was missing.

For the next seventeen years, people all over the territory reported seeing Billy wandering the hills. On several occasions, posses were organized to search for the dead outlaw, and once an entire cavalry troop took up the chase. But the only thing any of them ever found were dead bodies, some shot, some torn apart. In 1908, Pat Garrett was murdered by a gunshot to the head. The authorities arrested a man named Jesse Brazel for the crime. During his trial, Brazel claimed to have witnessed Billy the Kid fire the fatal shot. The judge struck Brazel's testimony from the record, but the jury took less than thirty minutes to find Brazel not guilty.

On the same day that Brazel's trial ended, the body of Billy the Kid was rediscovered in its grave. In 1940 the United States government erected a steel cage over Billy's grave. On the governmental requisition form in the box labeled "reason for expenditure" are the words "just in case." The most complete account of the second life of Billy the Kid can be found in the book *Re-killing Billy the Kid* by C. Upson.

Photos of Billy the Kid's grave as it looks today, still protected by its steel cage.

Artwork by Travis Ingram

other zombie varieties. Nor do most revenants display the hideous wounds that are common among horde zombies.

All of that said, at close range few revenants will be mistaken for one of the living. Their skin is unnaturally pale, their blood having congealed and often pooled into their feet. This often leads to a tightening of the skin, most noticeable around the fingernails and mouth, giving the impression they have claws and fangs. The tongue and the inside of the mouth have usually turned black. However, it is the eyes that have received most attention in the various accounts of revenant attacks. Where most zombies have blank, lifeless eyes, the eyes of a revenant seem to burn with a malignant intelligence, almost appearing to glow in some accounts.

These notable features have often caused revenants to be misidentified as vampires, a potentially deadly mistake. Revenants suffer from none of a vampire's weaknesses. While revenants do tend to shun direct sunlight, it doesn't cause them any ill effect. They can cross running water, eat garlic if they are so inclined, shrug off injuries from silver weapons, and even check themselves out in a mirror. Staking a revenant through the heart is likely to make it even angrier, but it won't slow it down. There is some evidence that revenants have difficulty crossing thresholds into private or religious buildings, but there is no consistent agreement on this among scholars.

The most important fact to note about revenants is that they are intelligent. They possess all of the knowledge they did in life, including specific skills and tool usage. While they may no longer possess the manual dexterity for origami, they can certainly pull the trigger of a gun, and, unlike necromantic zombies, revenants can both aim and reload. If a revenant commonly used weapons in its natural life, it will continue to do so in death and with only a slightly lessened ability.

Death does, at least, seem to cost revenants some of their perception. Although significantly more alert than their brain-dead cousins, revenants generally suffer from poor vision, dulled hearing, and a complete lack of taste and smell. While this can, and certainly should be used to the advantage of those hunting a revenant, it can lead to overconfidence. Just because the zombie cannot see that well does not mean it can be fooled by simple tricks. Some revenants have shown a marked ability for sensing a trap and turning the tables on their hunters.

Finally, revenants are able to speak. Due to dried throats and swollen tongues, they are often difficult to understand, however, with words coming out in a garbled rasp. While there is no point trying to reason with a revenant, it is often useful to try to understand what the zombie is saying, as it will likely give some indication of its motivation – information that can prove important in their destruction.

PREVENTION AND ELIMINATION

Revenants do not die easily. Whatever internal power brought them back to life will also keep them moving in the face of massive physical damage. There have been several cases of revenants being literally blown apart, and still the various parts struggled on.[10] Like all undead, revenants do not feel pain, nor do they suffer trauma or shock. However, alone among zombie types, revenants do have a basic sense of self-preservation. They will "run away to fight another day" if they are badly outnumbered or suspect a trap, but only for as long as it takes them to regroup or regain the upper hand.

Like necromantic zombies, revenants do not need brains, their own or anyone else's. Many a novice zombie fighter has died after scoring a perfect zombie head shot on a revenant. In fact, guns are nearly useless against a revenant, unless the shooter can manage to completely blow the head off the creature or saw through its neck with automatic fire.

Decapitation remains a revenant's only weak point, and even then it is not fatal. The removal or destruction of the head of a revenant causes a temporary paralysis in the creature. This will usually last for no more than a few minutes, after which time all of the pieces of the body will again reanimate. Depending on the revenant, some will continue to operate in multiple pieces, while others will attempt to gather their pieces back together. One account even has the revenant sewing his severed head back onto the stump of his neck.[11]

Artwork by Bill Reinhold

---

10 Despite many rumors and reports to the contrary, revenants are the only zombie type whose severed limbs often continue to move independently of the rest of the corpse for more than a few seconds.

11 Found in Chapter 32 of L. Murdick's *Memoirs*. The unpublished manuscript is held in the special collections department of Appalachian University.

There are only two ways to permanently stop a revenant. The first is appeasement. A revenant that has fulfilled its drive will eventually return to its grave and rest. Where the drive is in quest of a specific object, it is often best to just give the object to them. (After all, the irrational desire to possess it is what created the revenant in the first place.) Where a revenant is on a quest for blood, either for revenge or general anger, more drastic means must be used. To destroy a revenant, it must be totally obliterated. Certainly there are plenty of means to accomplish this – fire, acid, throwing them in

DRAUGR

In most ancient and medieval societies, discussions of the undead were considered taboo and in some cases heresy. For that reason more than any other, few tales of ancient zombies have survived to the present day in any complete form. However, the Vikings are a notable exception, and many of their stories contain encounters with various forms of undead. While the stories of the zombie-like *draugr* must be read with a skeptical eye, the similarities between these creatures and revenants seem too close to be coincidental.

Sometimes called *aptrgangr*, meaning "after-goer," the *draugr* are literally walking corpses. While they tend to show few signs of decay, their skin is normally described as either "black as death" or "corpse-pale." *Draugr* are also often described as giants or able to change their size at will. Some animate necrologists have argued that this could be the result of corpse bloating, but it is perhaps more likely a simple literary device to explain the strength and toughness of these creatures. Certainly there is no other corporeal undead that has ever shown such an ability.

In the sagas, the motivations of *draugr* are rarely explained, as they are often presented merely as a foil for the hero. That said, most have a tendency to haunt a specific area or continuously attack one family or village. Considering the commonality of blood feuds in medieval Norse society, it is easy to see these "hauntings" as the continuation of a feud from beyond the grave, an idea that fits well with the drive of most revenants.

There is one subvariety of *draugr*, the *haugbui*, or "mound-dweller," that displays a very clear drive. These creatures always stay in, or very near to, their burial mound in order to guard their burial treasure. While it is nowhere stated in the sagas, it is likely that these *haugbui* were notably greedy or miserly individuals in life, persons who valued the accumulation of wealth above all other things. It is a sad but not uncommon formula still occasionally seen in modern revenants.

Despite their literary flourishes, the Norse were a practical people, and if they didn't always explain the origins or motivations of *draugr*, they were at least clear on how to dispose of them. Since normal weapons were mostly ineffective against *draugr*, the heroes of the sagas generally had to wrestle them into submission; a fine idea for your ancient Viking heroes, a particularly bad idea for any modern hunter. Once the *draugr* was subdued, the Vikings would cut the head off it, which seems to have caused temporary paralysis much as it does with modern revenants. The two pieces of the *draugr* would then be burned down to ashes and these ashes were then buried or tossed into the sea.

Complete incineration – it worked for the Vikings; it still works today.

Previous page: Revenant

In the animate necrology community, the terms "reanimate" and "reawaken" have distinct meanings. A corpse reanimates when it becomes a zombie through magical, chemical, or viral means. Revenants, on the other hand, are said to reawaken due to their greater intelligence and awareness. Most revenants reawaken within a year of their death, but this is by no means a certainty. The record for the longest period of "initial death dormancy" is held by the World War II Japanese soldier, Tadamichi Giichi, who died on Okinawa in 1945 and returned to battle the Allies again in 1992.

volcanoes, and nuclear detonation all work, but rarely are these practical in the field. For that reason, experienced revenant hunters will either attempt to lure the target into some sort of holding cell or go for decapitation. Once decapitated, the creature can be bound in either chains or metal cable (rope is not strong enough), and then quickly transported to the nearest disposal facility, normally a crematorium.

Cremation also serves as the best form of prevention; ashes do not reanimate. Otherwise, preventing a revenant remains incredibly difficult. Despite vast amounts of research, predicting who will return as a revenant remains a fool's game. Even if you did know or suspect a specific person will return, if you aren't willing to cremate the body, then the next best thing is to wrap it in the strongest chains available, a rather tough sell to the next of kin.

In the final analysis, there is little that can be done to prevent revenants. Even if they are not fully understood, they seem to be a natural part of this world. We can only deal with each one individually as and when they claw their way up out of the ground.

Atomic Zombies

The world changed on July 16, 1945, the day that Robert J. Oppenheimer and his team test-fired the "Gadget" on the White Plains Proving Ground in New Mexico. The detonation of that first nuclear bomb heralded in an "Atomic Age" for mankind, but it also caused a subtle change in the chemical makeup of the planet. Through means that are still not clearly understood, the nuclear explosions of 1945 caused an "excitement" in the molecules of the atmosphere. This in turn excited the water vapor in the air,

Artwork by Charlie Adlard from *The Walking Dead*

which fell to earth, infecting the rivers and seas and eventually the ground itself. The effect was not a cataclysm as some had predicted, but a slight change to the physical and chemical laws of nature. It changed the boiling point and freezing point of water by one-hundredth of a degree. It made certain types of metal alloys impossible to cast. And perhaps most importantly, it brought about the birth of a new variety of zombie.

The term "atomic zombie" is slightly misleading. The explosion of the first atom bomb did not create any zombies, nor did the bombs dropped on Japan. Instead, they affected the world in such a way that future chemical processes would produce zombies. In fact, "chemical zombie" would probably be a more accurate term. While radiation remains the most common stimulus for an atomic zombie outbreak, it is not necessary. Nor are most atomic zombies radioactive (see notes below on "irradiated zombies"). For example, the Amazon River basin has seen several atomic zombie outbreaks due to certain combinations of nonradioactive industrial sludge being dumped into the river. Still, perhaps the "Atomic Age" deserves its own zombie, and by now the term is in common usage and would be difficult to change.

There are many who argue that 1945 was the most important year in the war against the undead, as it marked a vital turning point. With the defeat of Nazi Germany, the forces of necromancy were scattered far and wide, and many of its premier practitioners were killed. Yet out of the ashes of World War II a new threat

IRRADIATED ZOMBIES

While various forms of radiation can play a hand in the creation of an atomic zombie, most of these undead are themselves inert. However, because zombies are immune to all but the most powerful forms of radiation, it is possible for them to become irradiated. Irradiated zombies, or "rad zombies" for short, are walking dead that have been exposed to dangerous levels of radiation and now carry that radiation inside their lifeless shell. Depending on the level of irradiation, these zombies can burn or blister flesh with their touch or even with their breath. Even low-level rad zombies are incredibly dangerous, as prolonged exposure in their vicinity can lead to radiation sickness, cancer, and death.

The first reports of rad zombies came from Russia during the Gulag Uprisings. Sensing crisis, the Soviet military attempted to employ targeted nuclear weapons to stop the threat. Although these weapons effectively fried zombies within a limited "lethal zone," the fallout irradiated most of the rest. Since the military didn't realize this at the time, huge numbers of soldiers were exposed and died needless, painful deaths due to radiation poisoning. Since then, most countries have removed nuclear weapons from their anti-zombie arsenal. These days, rad zombies are most commonly found in the vicinity of nuclear power plants or nuclear waste dumps.

Becoming irradiated appears to have little or no effect on the zombie. It becomes neither stronger nor weaker. Theoretically, any type of zombie is capable of becoming irradiated, though to date there have been no reports of revenant or necromantic rad zombies.

Due to the ongoing possibility of rad zombies, most government-sponsored zombie-hunter teams now carry Geiger counters as standard equipment.

arose, a nightmare not born of human evil, but of the seemingly random misapplication of science. The zombie threat no longer hid in the shadows, but instead, it waited peacefully in graveyards and morgues. Its potential now hangs in the air all around us, waiting for a chemical spark to bring the dead back to their feet.

Artwork by Francis Tsai

Looking back, it is now apparent that atomic zombie outbreaks began as early as 1946. These proved to be small, isolated incidents. Most were written off as the work of rogue necromancers and quickly forgotten. Then, in the 1950s, rumors began to leak through the Iron Curtain of massive uprisings in the eastern gulags of the Soviet Union. The underground press was filled with sensationalist tales of prisoners going wild, tearing their guards apart with their teeth and hands, and even turning to cannibalism. The Soviet Union called it Western propaganda; the Free World hoped it marked the beginnings of a revolution. Only a few knew the truth. In 1958, the Soviet military surrounded and closed off the city of Magadan as part of a special "military maneuver." Only in the last year or two have a few accounts of the Magadan disaster made it to the Western world.

Meanwhile in America, a series of small outbreaks in California and Illinois alerted the scientific community to the fact that some new threat had arisen. With only sketchy reports and a few samples, a small group of universities worked together to found a new branch of science, Animate Necrology. While animate necrology would later encompass the study of necromancy and other varieties of the undead, it formed for the initial purpose of studying this new type of zombification. Many theories flew around in those early days. Some said it was a virus; others claimed that chemicals or radiation were eating away at the brains of the living, bringing on the appearance of death. The debate continued among this small community of scientists in America and abroad until 1968.

In 1968, an American satellite in low orbit hit a small piece of space dust and exploded over rural Pennsylvania. Over the next few days, the local press reported a spate of mass murders. The situation quickly spun out of control and the state government called in the National Guard to stabilize the situation. Officially the government has never commented on what happened in Pennsylvania in 1968, but many witnesses survived and have come forward to tell their stories.

It began in the hospitals and mortuaries. The recently dead stood up and attacked the living, stopping only to feast on those they had killed. As people died, they in turn rose up and joined the ranks of the zombies. Thousands died in less than a week, before the soldiers and local militia formed a cordon around the infected zone and, slowly tightening the circle, killed every zombie they could find.

Pennsylvania '68 is now a rallying cry for those in the animate necrology community. It is both proof of the dangers of atomic zombies and a test case for the effective overwhelming response needed to contain and eliminate a threat. Since 1968, the world has averaged nearly a dozen atomic zombie outbreaks a year. Most of these are small, and in the developed world they are quickly handled by specialist containment teams. However, the Third World remains extremely vulnerable to outbreaks, and it is often only with the assistance of the United Nations that an atomic zombie outbreak can be contained.

CREATION

The atomic blasts of 1945 left the world vulnerable to a particular form of contamination. The contamination can begin in either the air or water, but it will eventually spread from one to the other and into the ground as well. Unfortunately, the process of contamination is still only partially understood. It is a complex chemical reaction, often involving forms of extraterrestrial radiation. However, cases of contamination usually involve so many different chemical combination possibilities, that a true "source" has yet to be discovered. That, of course, assumes there is one source, and that contamination isn't achievable in multiple ways. In most cases, contamination can be traced back to the legal or illegal dumping of industrial waste combined with a particular cosmic event, although there is evidence that both have caused contamination on their own as well.

Artwork by Charlie Adlard from *The Walking Dead*

The area of contamination is highly variable, depending upon the spread of chemical waste and/or the power of radiation. To date, no charted contamination zone has covered more than 100 square miles. Thankfully, contamination zones have a limited duration. Most last only a couple of days, though a few have been known to carry on for weeks. Only the Chernobyl event has lasted more than a year, and it currently stands as the largest continuous zombie-contamination zone on record. Again, the reason behind the duration of a contamination zone is unknown. Scientists and animate necrologists rarely get to visit a "hot zone," and the Ukrainian authorities are still refusing to let international investigators near Chernobyl.

Since the process of contamination remains obscure, it has proved impossible to predict where a hot zone might spring up. That said, once an area has become contaminated, the spread of zombification follows a predictable pattern. Unlike necromantics, atomic zombies only form from the recently dead. As a general rule, around thirty days seems the cutoff point for a corpse to be reanimated by chemical means. By then, much of the internal tissue of the body and many organs have turned to mush and escaping gases have ruptured the skin. The first to be affected in a hot zone will be the most recently dead. Hospitals usually form ground zero for an atomic zombie outbreak. One moment everything is business as usual; in the next a man who just died on the operating table gets to his feet and attacks the surgeon. Within a few minutes of the contamination, the corpses in the hospital morgue also reanimate. In less than an hour, funeral parlors and crematoriums are also affected. By the end of the day, corpses will be battering their way out of mausoleums or digging themselves up from their graves.

There is a grim irony to outbreaks commonly starting in hospitals. Not only are they places where death and corpses are common, but they are also generally full of

Artwork by Charlie Adlard from *The Walking Dead*

ROBERT
HOT
BU
REAL
HONEST
FOOD

Previous pages: The Peoria Outbreak, 1958

One of the first major atomic zombie outbreaks in the United States occurred just outside the city of Peoria, Illinois in the spring of 1958. The contamination began when a nearby paper mill illegally dumped several vats of industrial waste in a creek near a family-owned graveyard. Soon after, three recently deceased members of the Jeffries clan clawed their way up from their graves and wandered into the city. Over the next thirty-six hours, the hordes swelled to over 100 zombies, including most of the members of the local high school football team. Local law-enforcement and emergency services eventually contained the outbreak before military help arrived. Over 150 people died during those three days of terror, not including the Jeffries family who were dead to begin with.

the ill and injured who can offer no resistance to an attacking zombie. Thus a single zombie can kill numerous people in a short space of time. These victims, now part of the recent dead, will also reanimate and join the rampage. In such a way, the number of zombies caused by contamination can easily multiply in the first few hours.

IDENTIFICATION AND THREAT

Because atomic zombies were the first zombie variety commonly accepted by the modern media, they have shaped the public perception of the undead threat. If you ask most individuals on the street to describe a zombie (and they don't run away), they will most likely describe an atomic zombie. Put simply, an atomic zombie looks like an upright corpse that happens to be wandering around. They are generally deathly pale, have vacant, slack-jawed expressions, and walk with a limping, shambling gait. They will often extend their arms, groping the air in front of them, trying to grasp any living thing that comes near. Even from a distance, anyone who has any knowledge of zombies should be able to recognize them by their odd stance and movement.

Atomic zombies have only one motivating factor: the need to feed.[12] While zombies have no metabolism as such, the chemical process that animates their corpses also slowly burns at the meat and tissue that holds the zombie together. Consuming more flesh gives the chemical process an alternate fuel source that will keep the zombie going. While no exact studies have been done, it is estimated that just a small handful of flesh or a small animal like a bird will keep a zombie going for at least a day or two.

In their quest for flesh, zombies wander aimlessly until something catches their attention. Atomic zombie eyesight is incredibly poor and is based on movement. They will react to anything that moves faster than their own shuffling walk. For the most part, these zombies rely on their hearing, which remains acute even in death. They generally notice any unusual sound louder than a slight breeze and will move in the direction of the noise. The louder the sound, the quicker they react (although "quick" is a very relative term here). Atomic zombies also possess a sense of smell, though this sense has only one setting. Once they are within a few feet of a living creature, zombies

[12] Contrary to popular mythology, zombies do not need to eat brains. This seems to be a confusion of the idea that an atomic zombie needs its own brain to function. Zombies will certainly eat brains, but show no preference for them.

can smell it. It remains unclear exactly what scent zombies smell, though sweat remains the strongest contender.[13]

Artwork by Chris Stevens

The smell of living prey triggers this type of zombie's famous "moan reflex." Those unlucky enough to have heard the moan of a zombie wish only to forget the experience. Many who have suffered from post-traumatic stress disorder relating to zombies have reported that it is the moan, more than anything else, that haunts their waking dreams. Zombies create this sound by pushing the excess gas generated by the chemical reaction up through their throats. The result is a dry, warbling groan that can be heard from several rooms away.

At first examination, the moan might seem a strange survival mechanism, as its only function is to attract other zombies toward food, thus forcing the original zombie to share. However, on further study, the moan is seen as a vital part of the zombie way of life (if you'll pardon the expression). Individual atomic zombies are slow and awkward and only able to catch the injured, frail, or particularly stupid. It is only through gathering together and attempting to surround prey that zombies can truly hope to capture their meal. The moan has such a powerful pull on zombies that they will sometimes leave a fresh kill in order to follow another moan.

The moan, then, becomes the vital tool in the gathering of a zombie horde. In scientific communities, any group of ten or more zombies is technically considered a horde, but most zombie hunters use the term to mean a much larger gathering. Otherwise, a horde is defined as any gathering of at least ten zombies where they are grouped closely enough that each member can hear the moan of at least three other members. When one zombie in a horde moans, the others will also, an effect that works like a lure to bring in zombies from all around. In cases of particularly large hordes, the cumulative sound of the moaning can reach painful volumes.

Even in a horde, atomic zombies are still mindless creatures. They do not employ any tactics *per se*. Surrounding their victims is only a happenstance of position and not a conceived plan. Despite this, a horde of zombies is extremely dangerous. Unlike their necromantic cousins, atomic zombies are incredibly strong. Since they feel no

---

[13] Thanks to Prof R. Sullivan's "Porcine Feed Experiments," blood has been ruled out as a zombie attractor.

pain, they will push their muscles past the limit. There have been cases where zombies have grabbed onto passing cars and had their arms ripped off at the shoulders rather than let go. In all cases it is best to stay as far away from an atomic zombie as possible. Once in their grip, it is difficult to escape, and their moan will soon attract others.

ELIMINATION AND PREVENTION

Thankfully, unlike necromantic zombies or revenants, atomic zombies have a clearly defined weakness. Despite their undead nature, atomic zombies still have one working organ: the brain. In the last few years, scientists have managed to conduct a number of neurological experiments on captured zombies. These tests have confirmed that while the creatures have no higher brain functions, no "thoughts" as we define them, their brains do coordinate and control their limited motor functions. If the zombie brain is destroyed, all motor functions cease, and the zombie deanimates, crumpling into a heap.

Destroy the brain and you destroy the zombie. In the late 1990s and the early years of the new millennium, this became the catchphrase of many amateur zombie-hunting societies. It appeared on T-shirts, bumper stickers, and key chains. As the internet grew in power and reach, the phrase traveled as fast and as far as email could carry it. It became an eight-word gospel, and many people died because of it.

Don't get me wrong, the knowledge is important, but the knowledge in isolation has two deadly shortcomings. First, as readers of this monograph will already be aware, the "destroy the brain" rule does not apply to all forms of zombies. It works for atomic and viral zombies but is less effective against necromantic zombies and revenants. Identify the zombie first, then determine the best way to dispatch it. However, even if you know you are facing an atomic zombie, there is a second problem. Destroying the brain isn't nearly as easy as it sounds.

Have you ever tried tossing a baseball in the air and hitting it with a bat? Most people, asked to do this for the first time, will swing and miss. In fact, many people will miss several times before they make contact. Now, imagine that baseball is coming at you with outstretched arms, a moan rasping from its blood-stained lips. Granted a zombie head is significantly bigger than a baseball, but it is also moving in an erratic pattern. The zombie isn't trying to dodge – they never do – but its broken-legged walk causes it to sway from side to side and up and down. You've got one shot with your bat. One swing to connect solidly with the skull with enough force to crack it open and smash the brains beneath. If you miss, if the shot glances off the skull, the zombie will wrap you in its arms and bite out your throat. In a matter of minutes, you will be one of them.

Photograph by Mike Slaby

ATOMIC ZOMBIES

BEST METHOD OF ELIMINATION: DESTROY THE BRAIN

The truth is, most people have not developed their hand-eye coordination to a point where they can hit a moving target solidly with any degree of consistency. Sadly, most people badly overestimate their own ability, and this has led to many needless deaths. Even for those trained in combat (or baseball), engaging in hand-to-hand combat against atomic zombies is never recommended. Remember, these creatures usually travel in hordes; even if you take down the first or second zombie, there will likely be more than you can kill. Where hand-to-hand fighting is unavoidable, kill only as many zombies as you need to clear a path and then run. Once you are out of their reach, they will not be able to catch you.

In all cases, atomic zombies should be eliminated from a distance, but even then it can be more difficult than first imagined. Hitting a small moving target with a bullet is incredibly difficult, especially under pressure. Also, only a direct hit will penetrate the skull, as evolution specifically designed it to deflect blows. Still, a solid shot through an eye or smack in the forehead will take down any atomic zombie. The effect is virtually instantaneous, almost like flipping an off switch. The zombie immediately ceases all forward movement and collapses.

Because of the atomic zombie's weakness, it is particularly easy to prevent, even if the prevention is just as distasteful as the cure. A corpse with a destroyed (or removed) brain will not reanimate due to chemical conditions. While most morticians are aware of the zombie threat, few will apply this simple preventive measure unless it is specifically requested. Where the next of kin does request zombie-proofing, or more commonly if it is stated in the will of the deceased, the mortician will drive a long, thin nail called a skull pick through the crown of the skull down into the brain. It is quick, mostly clean, and completely painless (assuming the recipient is actually dead).

For those afraid of having nails in their head after they die, there is always cremation, which prevents all forms of zombie reanimation. If neither of these options is acceptable, bodies can be buried in a metal coffin. While this will not prevent reanimation, when combined with six feet of earth, it will prevent even the most determined atomic zombie from breaking out, leaving the unfortunate corpse to slowly consume itself.

Viral Zombies

As early as the mid-1960s, a few within the animate necrology community described the zombie threat as a virus. With necromantic, revenant, and atomic zombies, the undead seemed to continuously evolve, offering new threats just as humanity came to grips with the old ones. Then, sometime in the early 1970s, the metaphor became a reality. Like most viruses, it is impossible to trace the zombie virus back to its origin, that point where an essentially benign biological agent mutated into one of the greatest dangers of the twenty-first century.

Most necrovirologists agree that the first strands of the virus developed in China. However, because of China's strict media control, doubts remain as to the exact time and location of the initial outbreaks. The first confirmed report comes from 1972, when a group of American and Canadian backpackers became entangled in an outbreak near the Tibet border. The Chinese authorities held the backpackers in prison on supposed visa violations for nearly a year before bowing to international pressure for their release. Upon their return to North America, the outbreak survivors told their tale to anyone who would listen.[14] For over six months, the story made the rounds through television and newspapers but was eventually lost in the noise from the Watergate scandal.

Unfortunately, the problem did not go away. Instead, it spread. In 1977 several outbreaks occurred in remote parts of Vietnam. By 1980, almost every country in Asia had experienced at least one undead event. In those early days, most people didn't recognize the virus as a form of zombification. Working with only limited data, virologists assumed it to be a new strain of *Lyssavirus*, the family which includes rabies. It was not until the mid-1980s that specialists realized that virus victims were, in fact, dead. The victims still walked around and tried to attack other people, but by almost every other factual indicator their bodies had died. Their hearts stopped beating. They didn't breathe. Their brains showed no activity beyond basic sensory response and motor control. No hint of a personality remained.

By this point, the virus, now sometimes called the Z-virus, had spread to Africa and Eastern Europe. As it began to enter North Atlantic Treaty Organization (NATO)-protected territory, knowledge of the virus spread quickly through government

[14] For the most complete account of the unfortunate backpackers see *Through the Land of the Dead* by Abe Davies, Yukon Ink, 1974.

and military channels. Thankfully, previous outbreaks had been small and successfully contained, though more through luck than any coordinated response. Since most First World nations already maintained zombie-containment teams to combat earlier threats, they retrained them to tackle this new menace.

In 1994, the world witnessed its first mass outbreak of zombies in the suburbs of Mexico City. At first, the violence was mistaken for a massive drug war between rival clans. By the time the true danger had been ascertained, thousands had been infected and rampaged through the city. Despite the brave battle fought by the Mexican "Zorros" Special Forces, the government pleaded for outside assistance. Within twenty-four hours, a multinational task force headed by the Americans landed outside the city. The battle of Mexico City lasted for nearly four days, as anti-zombie forces scoured the city, eliminating the infected. When the smoke finally cleared, 37,000 people had died, including an unknown number of task force soldiers.

While the feeble cover-up allowed most of the world's population to dismiss the whole situation, people in power realized that the zombie threat had reached new levels. In the last twenty years, there have been no fewer than 342 confirmed viral zombie outbreaks, and who knows how many more have gone unreported. Incredibly, much of the world is still only slowly waking up to this massing threat. While no subsequent outbreak has reached anywhere near the level of Mexico City, many believe it is only a matter of time.

Artwork by Charlie Adlard from *The Walking Dead*

CREATION

The Z-virus lives in the blood and tissue of the human body. It can be spread in two ways. First, it can be accidentally ingested. It is theorized that most viral zombie outbreaks begin with one individual either eating infected food or drinking contaminated water. It takes only a minuscule amount of infected tissue to taint a new host. Once infected, the host can live anywhere from one hour to a day and a half, depending on the strength of the virus and the determination of the host. During this time, the host develops severe flu-like symptoms, becoming pale and weak until death finally claims them. After death, it is only a matter of minutes before the now-lifeless corpse reanimates. The new zombie immediately seeks out others to infect, which leads to the second, more common way, the virus is spread.

Like most living organisms, the Z-virus has the overriding goal to live and to reproduce. Using its new host corpse, the virus attempts to spread itself by attacking noninfected humans. To spread, the virus must penetrate a victim's skin and infect the tissue beneath, which can be done with a quick bite or rake with fingernails. A wound that draws blood carries a nearly 100 percent chance of infection.

Viral zombies are not cannibalistic. Although they often attack with their mouths and may occasionally get a bit overenthusiastic in their efforts to infect prey, they do not need to ingest flesh or anything else to survive. As of yet, science has no explanation for what viral zombies use as a power source. So, unlike atomic zombies, viral zombies often infect a host, leave him or her wounded, and quickly move on to the next target. Because of this methodology, viral zombie outbreaks can rapidly and exponentially expand. In truth, it is this expansion potential that is their biggest threat, and why it is imperative that outbreaks be quickly identified and contained.

IDENTIFICATION AND THREAT

One of the main reasons it took science so long to identify viral zombies as a separate classification is that the initial specimens appeared so similar in character to atomic zombies. All of the Chinese and Vietnamese outbreaks featured slow, moaning zombies. With their containment and elimination, few further tests were conducted. But as the years passed and the virus spread, different zombie outbreaks showed a worrying degree of individualism. Some zombies moved and reacted quicker. Others showed slightly more intelligence. Now, science understands this to be the result of Z-virus mutation. Today, there are 47 different recognized strands of Z-virus, and each produces a different variety of zombie. Luckily, even with this variation, all viral zombies still show enough similarities that they can be discussed under

Artwork by Sina Kazemian

the same classification. In fact, the differences generally manifest as varying levels of speed and intelligence and not as any truly unique features.

As mentioned, the first viral zombies mimicked atomic zombies in almost every way, except that they were not cannibalistic and reproduced through infection. These early viral zombies do still occasionally crop up, but their threat has mostly been contained. It is the newer "fast zombies" that now pose the greatest threat. Often called "aggressor zombies" in hunter circles, these undead are the most human-looking of all zombie varieties. At a distance it is nearly impossible to distinguish them from the living. A closer inspection reveals them to be unnaturally pale, with eyes rolled back into their heads. They almost always keep their mouths open and their teeth bared. In fact, the easiest way of recognizing a viral zombie, especially an aggressor, is how it charges directly at the nearest living person.

Artwork by Travis Ingram

At the highest end yet recorded, aggressor zombies can run as fast as a living person. Moreover, with no functioning respiratory system or pain receptors, they are able to maintain a top sprinting speed for longer than most humans. In a straight footrace, aggressor zombies nearly always win. The same applies to hand-to-hand combat. These zombies can push their muscles to the limit longer than most humans. Considering that viral zombies only need to inflict a blood-wound, hand-to-hand combat should be avoided at all costs.

Viral zombies do not use weapons. It is unclear if this is due to a lack of intelligence or just a function of their drive to spread infection. There are no reports of them using tools of any kind, and like most other zombies, they will continuously ram themselves against a door in order to break it down without ever attempting to turn a doorknob. That said, unlike atomic zombies, some of the more aggressive viral zombies can climb. They will not attempt to scale the side of a building or anything tricky, but will happily launch themselves up and over any small wall or fence that stands in a direct line between them and their prey.

Most viral zombies have decent sensory perception. Their eyesight is poor and mostly based on movement, but their hearing and sense of smell remain as acute as in life. Some varieties of viral zombie moan and respond to moans in much the same way as their atomic cousins, but this is less and less common. Most viral zombies, and almost all aggressor types, do not moan. Despite this, they still possess a type of herd mentality. Viral zombies tend to band together in order to hunt prey and often react to one another. Viral zombie herd mentality remains a hotly debated topic among necrovirologists, with numerous credible but conflicting theories competing for space in the journals.

Artwork by Alan Gallo

ELIMINATION AND PREVENTION

Despite their great speed and strength, viral zombies remain slightly more susceptible to physical damage than most zombies. While a single shotgun blast to the chest will not take one out, multiple blasts often do the trick. Alternatively, a fully automatic assault rifle can tear them apart. Such methodology does require a heavy expenditure of ammunition and is relatively slow. Luckily, like atomic zombies, all varieties of viral zombie are vulnerable to the destruction of the brain. One clean head shot will take them down, and this remains the favored technique of most hunters. It should be noted however, that the increased speed of aggressor zombies can make this a very difficult shot indeed.

Humanity also possesses one weapon in the war on viral zombies that it doesn't have for other types: anti-viral drugs. In 2002, Dr Hall Moore and his team at the University of Maryland created the first viable anti-Z-virus drug. While the drug could not be turned into a vaccine, it could be applied to a newly infected host before death, and it gave the victim at least a 50 percent chance at survival. Today, this drug has been improved to 90 percent effectiveness if applied within the first hour.

Mankind cannot grow over-dependent on this miracle drug. The Z-virus is a constantly mutating and evolving entity. It needs to be continuously studied and the anti-viral drugs modified to keep pace. Also, this anti-virus remains expensive to produce and difficult to store. For now, it remains the domain of governments and their containment teams.

Other than the hope for more and better drugs, there is little mankind can do to prevent viral zombies. Governments must focus on quick containment of outbreaks; individuals should try their best not to get bitten.

VIRAL ZOMBIES

BEST METHOD OF PREVENTION:
ANTI-Z-VIRUS DRUG

Zombie Masters

Many within the scientific community will scoff at my inclusion of a section on zombie masters, but considering the rising tide of evidence, I believe it would be neglectful not to at least discuss the possibility of their existence. Traditionally, the term "zombie master" was irregularly applied to necromancers who had assembled a large force of zombie minions, but in the last decade it has become more commonly associated with a possible viral zombie phenomenon. Today's zombie master generally refers to a zombie Typhoid Mary, a living human who carries the zombie virus.

To date, no official study can confirm the existence of a human carrier. In fact, according to the official record, no one has ever survived infection from a zombie virus without the quick application of an anti-virus. But a lack of scientific documentation does not mean human carriers don't exist. In the last ten years, there have been more than a dozen zombie survivor accounts that at least hint at the possibility. The first comes from the diary of Joanna Blitch, who survived for 12 days inside an office building during the 2002 "Mooresville Outbreak":

> *...overnight Casey turned into one of them, but was killed before she could hurt anyone else. Casey had never been touched by one of them, never bitten or clawed. But just the day before she'd applied bandages to Kevin's arm after he'd cut himself on the glass. People began to talk, to say that Kevin must be infected, even though he showed no signs. During the debate, Kevin ran for the door and flung himself out into the night. We waited to hear his screams, but there was only silence.*[15]

Certainly this account is far from conclusive, but it is just one of several that tell a similar story. One of the most famous comes from Matthew Wright, who survived an outbreak in the English Midlands:

> *I saw him standing there, surrounded by zombies, a terrifying smile on his face. It was clear he wasn't one of them. He still had intelligence in his eyes. But they didn't attack him. At first, they seemed to crowd around him to protect him. Then he raised his hand and pointed at us, and the zombies began to charge.*

[15] From the unpublished diary of Joanna Blitch, which resides in the author's collection.

Artwork by David Machuca

Mr Wright's account[16] is notable for two reasons; first because it was the first account to be corroborated by independent witnesses, but more importantly, it introduced a new possibility to the world of zombie studies. In none of the varied accounts of possible zombie Typhoid Marys is the suspected carrier killed by zombies. In fact, in several cases, including Mr Wright's, the zombies seem to protect and even *obey* the carrier.

The implications of a human mind controlling a viral zombie horde is worrisome in the extreme, and that has perhaps led some within the community to stick their heads in the sand and deny the possibility without a thorough investigation. Despite the admitted lack of concrete evidence, the only counter-argument seems to hinge on the impossibility of communication between a living human and a viral zombie. Of course, this argument overlooks the ongoing debate about the viral hive mind.

As discussed in the previous chapter, some varieties of viral zombie do not moan, and yet they still seem to move in the same direction and "respond" to other zombies that have identified potential prey. Whether this is the result of some kind of psychic connection or has a more tangible scientific explanation, there seems no good reason that a human carrier of the virus might not also be incorporated into this hive mind. If this were the case, the complex, individualistic human mind might easily come to dominate the narrow thinking of a zombie horde.

16 *Never Again: An Outbreak Survivor's Tale*, Dark Asylum Press, 2004.

Previous pages: The Toronto Frenzy

Despite the huge number of zombie outbreaks in the US, Canada has been relatively untouched by the zombie menace. However in 2007, a small viral outbreak occurred in Toronto resulting in 132 deaths. During this incident, several witness identified a red-coated woman directing the zombies. Later identified as Katherine Flint, this mysterious individual appeared during two further zombie outbreaks in the United States, evading capture both times. She has quickly risen to near the top of the FBI's Most Wanted list, and remains the strongest evidence for a living zombie master.

Of course, this is all conjecture at this point, and I don't want to overstate the case. I do want to make it clear that the possibility of such zombie masters should be considered, and all zombie hunters should be on the lookout. Should a true zombie master ever be encountered in the field, all efforts should be directed at its immediate elimination. As much as science would relish the chance to study a live specimen, the danger of human intelligence guiding a zombie outbreak is too great a risk.

Viral Hounds and Other Zombified Animals

In 1982, Sgt E. Moore of the British 77th Division reported the existence of a pack of viral zombie hounds terrorizing villagers in the backwoods of Bulgaria. This report revived an old debate within the animate necrology community about the commonality and classification of zombified animals, a debate which continues to the present. While some scientists believe that a new branch of study should be opened to focus solely on undead animals, others, this author included, believe that animals should be viewed as members of one of the already existent zombie classifications. In nearly every case, zombie animals display the same strengths and weakness of a human corpse of the same zombie type. To lump all zombie animals into one category could cause confusion and do a major disservice to the men and women who risk their lives combating the zombie threat.

Artwork by Marissa "Llawlietdeathnote" Evans

USAF

Getty Images

Two dogs infected with the Z-virus.

The story of zombie animals begins with the ancient necromancers. Theoretically, a sufficiently powerful necromancer can reanimate the body of any creature as a zombie. However, there seems little point in the exercise. Reanimated animals retain few of the advantages they possessed in life. Even the larger mammals become slow, weak creatures, neither significantly stronger nor tougher than a human zombie. True, necromantic fish can swim and some undead birds can fly, but it takes an extremely imaginative necromancer to make use of such ineffectual servants. For the most part, necromancers reanimate animals more for vanity than anything else. Perhaps a skeletal mastodon is a status symbol in the necromantic community. Some necromancers do use an undead animal as a sort of grim familiar, though to what end is unknown.

Interestingly, wielders of voodoo black magic are not able to create any zombie animals. Voodoo zombification requires the incarceration of the *zombi astral*, the soul of the deceased. Since animals do not possess souls, or at least not in the same way as humans, there is nothing for a bokor to imprison. Many bokors have other spells they use to enchant animals, but such magic is beyond this investigation.

The possibility of animal revenants remains an intriguing one, but there are no clear-cut cases to date. There are several reports of dogs that have exhibited signs of revenant behavior or appearance, but so far every case has ended with the destruction of the animal in question, so no true studies have been possible.[17]

It was only with the dawn of the atomic zombie that animals became true participants in the zombie curse, and then only on a limited scale. As science is still trying to determine exactly how various chemical interactions lead to the reanimation of corpses, it cannot at this time say why certain species are vulnerable and others are not. In fact, it may be that a specific chemical reaction only causes the reanimation of certain species, and that we only tend to notice when that species is human or another large mammal. Luckily, atomic zombie animals mimic their human cousins and become slow, sluggish creatures.[18] Although dangerous, these undead animals have proven only a minimal threat to humanity, unlike their cousins, the viral hounds.

[17] The most famous case is the 1889 "Moor Hound Incident."

[18] For a full list of creatures reanimated through chemical means see Dr M. Ramalho's paper *The Unextinction Agenda*.

Previous page: Viral hounds

Unlike their human counterparts, zombie canines do possess a vague sense of hierarchy. Most zombie dog packs contain an alpha male, a dog that the others follow. These alpha males direct and guide their pack through a series of growls and barks that function in much the same way as zombie moaning.

While it has not been conclusively proven, zombie dogs show a predilection for attacking other dogs before attacking humans. Some mercenary containment units employ their own (living) dogs to act as bait should they encounter a zombie dog pack.

There is perhaps a sick irony that the only species besides humans to be affected by the zombie viruses is man's best friend, but the truth is no joke.[19] As incredibly dangerous as viral zombies can be, they are nothing compared to the four-legged variety. Blessed with the natural speed and powerful jaws of many dog breeds, viral hounds strike like undead missiles, covering ground at an incredible rate and snapping at exposed flesh with infected teeth.

While neither viral zombies nor viral hounds employ true tactics, the two groups often unintentionally work together to trap living targets. The speed of the hounds means they always outpace human zombies, reaching the target first. These swift attackers invariably force the living to seek shelter in either a building or a vehicle. While this shelter does provide protection from the hounds, it leaves people vulnerable to the zombies following close behind who will likely batter their way inside.

Viral hounds can be eliminated through the destruction of the brain, but their speed and low profile make delivering such a blow difficult. Professional zombie hunters, when faced with a viral hound situation, almost always use vehicles in the first instance. Armored cars with battering rams or even snowplows make good weapons against viral hounds. Driving through a pack at high speed will usually mangle most of the hounds to such a degree that their speed advantage will be neutralized and they can be finished off at a leisurely pace.

Finally, a note on crows and other carrion fowl. It is not unusual to see birds pecking at the infected flesh of viral zombies (or any other type of zombie). While I can find no recorded case of birds becoming infected with the virus, eating zombie flesh has been known to cause aggressive, almost rabid behavior in birds – to the point that they will sometimes attack humans. These attacks are extremely dangerous as the birds strike from the sky and often go for a target's eyes. However, wounds caused in such an attack are not infected. To date, no one has ever received a zombie virus through a bird attack. Still, this is just one more reason why strong eye protection is necessary when fighting in an infection zone.

[19] New research indicates that several primate species may also be vulnerable to the viruses.

Zombie Hunters

Over the last two decades, the term "zombie hunter" has become diluted by the increasing number of amateur groups who seem determined to die in as gruesome a manner as possible. Theoretically, it is a problem that should take care of itself, but for every hick with a shotgun who gets his throat bitten out, it seems two more want to take his place. I have neither the time nor the inclination to talk about these groups. My interest is in the trained professionals who devote their lives to combating the zombie menace.

The first true zombie hunters probably date back to the days of prehistory, but aside from a few fables and legends, their stories have been lost to us. During the Crusades, several knightly orders formed for the express purpose of battling the undead, but if any true accounts of their activities survive, they are buried deep in the Vatican's *Corpus Mortuambulanticum*. In fact, despite the long history of zombies, the story of zombie hunting can only really be traced back to the mid-eighteenth century, with the formation of the Honourable Society of the Resurrection Men.

HONOURABLE SOCIETY OF THE RESURRECTION MEN

Generally, "Resurrection Men" refers to British body-snatchers of the eighteenth century, people who stole corpses and sold them to medical colleges. While technically illegal, the penalty for body-snatching was only a small fine, which was far outweighed by the potential profit. The trade became so popular, especially in Scotland, that it eventually attracted several necromancers who saw body-snatchers as easy supply men for zombie experiments. By the early 1750s, Edinburgh had become the necromantic capital of the world, and deaths due to zombie attack had reached unprecedented levels. While some body-snatchers grew wealthy supplying the necromancers, others turned against the trade. In 1756, an unknown Edinburgh body-snatcher founded the Honourable Society of the Resurrection Men in order to fight back. Because the society used an illegal practice to disguise their efforts to protect the public, the true identities of these first zombie hunters remain unknown. However, some of their *noms de plume* have become legendary: Mr Thomas Bones, Jonas Teeth Esq, Madame Noir Bent and

Artwork by Marc Lee

of course, Stanley Barrett, the cyclopean artist, whose disturbing one-eyed painting style has landed his works in museums throughout Europe and America.

For decades the society waged a vigilante war against the necromancers and their body-snatcher helpers. Both sides suffered numerous casualties, but while necromancer numbers slowly dwindled, the society grew, gaining members in high places. Eventually, the society won the war, not on the streets of Edinburgh, but in the Houses of Parliament. In 1832, Parliament passed the Anatomy Act, which changed the law regarding access to cadavers and effectively ended the body-snatching trade. Learning from this lesson, the society continued in its mission to stop necromancy but now used

THE ZOMBIE DUELING ASSOCIATION

Founded in the early years of the twenty-first century, the Zombie Dueling Association is an underground gladiatorial society which pits captured zombies against hired gladiators. Outlawed in every civilized country, the society holds secret events all over the world, including a yearly championship on a large ship in international waters. Zombies are supplied by several less-than-reputable mercenary organizations, while most of the gladiators come from the same place. However, occasionally gladiators are hired from professional sports, with former American Football players being in high demand. To become a member of the ZDA requires deep pockets, friends in the right places, and a complete lack of compunction. The ZDA is organized into a number of different clubs, each of which supply their own gladiators and zombies. It is estimated that there are over 300 members worldwide.

Previous page: "The LA Bust-out"

In 2009, the United States experienced its largest and most public viral zombie outbreak in downtown Los Angeles. Over a period of four days, members of the US Army's 34th Regiment barricaded eighteen city blocks and launched a series of reconnaissance and rescue missions into the infected area. Dubbed the "LA Bust-out" by the media, the mission proved a huge success and for the first time brought the US Army's specialist zombie hunters into the public eye.

research and legal pressure as its main weapons. The Honourable Society of the Resurrection Men has survived to the present, and is now a pan-European organization dedicated to the elimination of all forms of zombie. However, as is wise for amateur organizations, they leave the actual combat to trained professionals.

BUREAU 9

The story of professional government zombie-hunting teams begins during the American Civil War. As mentioned previously, this war included a huge rise in necromantic activity. Realizing that the Union faced a threat perhaps even greater than the Confederacy, Abraham Lincoln asked the head of his bodyguard, Allan Pinkerton, to establish a new bureau to combat the problem. Pinkerton in turn gave the task to two of his most trusted men, Agents Rufus Thurston and Roland Briscoe. These two men established "Bureau 9," a hand-picked team of agents who traveled the country undercover, eliminating necromantic threats. The men usually worked in pairs. One agent served mainly as the investigator, identifying and studying potential threats. The second man carried the gun.

Artwork by Fab for KOEMZO DESIGN

After the war, President Andrew Johnson decided the bureau should continue its work. Records from this time are still classified and will probably remain so indefinitely. Still, it is well known that Bureau agents continued their work outside of the United States, traveling all through North, South, and Central America, and played a major part in the US interventions in Haiti. During World War II, the agents participated in many activities of the Shadow Theater. Today, Bureau 9 continues its work as a joint project of the FBI and CIA. Their main targets remain necromancers and bokors, but their activities also cover other zombie threats. Unlike the old days, however, when a serious threat arises they turn over operations to the military.

THE CONTAINMENT TEAMS

While the zombie problem remained mostly necromantic in nature, governments deemed it best to have small organizations such as Bureau 9 deal with the threat and only call out the military in extreme circumstances. But with the rise of atomic zombies after World War II, a new solution became necessary. No longer could zombie situations be resolved with one well-placed bullet. Only boots on the ground could lay down enough firepower to stop a full outbreak.

The Vatican City was the first country to officially establish anti-zombie forces in 1955, and many countries still send observers to see these specialist members of the Swiss Guard in action. However, these teams have limited reach and are only rarely deployed. The real advent of the military zombie hunters came in 1963 with the NATO "Containment Ordinance." This small reorganization of military forces established specialist "Containment Teams" that could deploy quickly to suppress any zombie outbreak. These teams were multinational forces, with members drawn from all NATO countries. Containment team members received special training in combating zombies (all varieties) and specialist gear (see next chapter). While NATO still maintains a number of containment teams that can be deployed by helicopter or airlift, almost all of the member nations have now established similar organizations within their own militaries.

In the United States, the "Nightmen" of the 34th Specialist Regiment are based at Fort Bragg. The regiment boasts nearly 1,500 troops, including specialist support staff, and a dedicated flight of Black Hawk helicopters. The United Kingdom recruits most

Some smaller countries employ special anti-zombie police units.

MERCENARY ORGANIZATIONS

With the vast increase in the zombie threat over the past two decades, a number of private military companies have seen an opening in the market. Call them "private zombie contractors" or "undead disposal specialists," they are essentially mercenaries who specialize in fighting zombies. Like standard mercenaries, the different groups vary greatly in both ability and reliability. Some of these so-called organizations are little more than "wannabe" zombie hunters with a couple of hunting rifles and an armored pickup truck. Others are multinational corporations who employ numerous former containment team soldiers and supply them with the latest military hardware. Since most First World nations support their own containment teams, mercenaries are most active in less-developed countries, with South America, Africa, and parts of Asia being their main stomping grounds.

To date the most successful and widely recognized of these organizations is *Command: The Blue Marble* (C:TBM). Originally established in South Africa in 1997, the group now supports bases in 19 different countries around the world. Under the leadership of Aloysius Wu, C:TBM has expanded its operations to cover nearly all forms of undead and other so-called "monsters," but battling zombie outbreaks remains their primary market. The group has a sterling reputation and an extremely high success rate, both of which are reflected in their top-of-the-market fees.

of its zombie hunters from the ranks of the Royal Marine Commandos, placing them in a unit known as Division 77, "The Dirge."

Today, most militaries contain at least a token zombie-hunting force, although the quality and training of these groups varies wildly. The United States and Britain maintain two of the best because, for reasons unknown, these countries suffer a much higher rate of zombie outbreaks *per capita* than anywhere else in the world.

OUTBREAK SURVIVORS

While they're not really "zombie hunters," I believe it is worth mentioning the men and women who unwittingly get caught up in zombie outbreaks. Unlike the amateur hunters mentioned at the opening of this chapter, these people do not go looking for a fight but are only doing what they must to survive.

There are several books on the market that attempt to educate people on how to survive a zombie outbreak. While some of these contain valuable information, they have also done much to propagate the "zombie survivor myth." There is nothing glamorous or glorious about being caught up in a zombie outbreak. It is a terrifying, chaotic battlefield. No matter how many books a person has read or how many hours they've clocked at the shooting range, the single biggest factor in survival is luck.

Even for the lucky few who do escape, most suffer from post-traumatic stress disorder and can spend the rest of their lives trying to recover. Psychology is only just

Artwork by Andrée Wallin

beginning to scratch the surface of the effects of seeing a friend or loved one turned into a walking corpse. The Zombie Wars are not a game.[20] While numerous civilians have been appropriately lauded as heroes for their actions during zombie outbreaks, they are greatly outnumbered by the piles of corpses left behind.

[20] See the Further Reading chapter for some great games relating to the zombie wars.

Zombie Hunter Weapons and Equipment

As with most modern military special forces, zombie hunters are allowed wide leeway to choose their own equipment. What follows is an overview of the most commonly employed weapons and equipment and the rationale behind their usage. This list is not meant to be exhaustive, nor is it a checklist for would-be zombie hunters. It is provided to give a better understanding of the desperate battles between the living and the undead.

FIREARMS

As explained earlier, guns are not always the most efficient zombie killers. However, since humanity hasn't invented a better ranged-weapon alternative, firearms remain the primary armament for all zombie hunters. Of course, some firearms are more effective than others. Most zombie hunters carry some form of carbine as their primary weapon. Slightly shorter and lighter than assault rifles but with the same toughness and reliability, carbines such as the American M4 make good short-range zombie-sniping weapons and can be loaded up with a huge range of accessories. In a standard four-man zombie containment fire team, it is usual for at least two men to carry carbines. Of the other two, one is often equipped with a longer-ranged target rifle. The fourth team member generally carries a military shotgun. Military shotguns such as the AA-12 are considered by many to be the

An AA-12 automatic shotgun.

US Marine Corps

ultimate anti-zombie weapon. With their low recoil, extreme hitting power, and decent-sized magazines, they can blow apart just about any zombie: magical, chemical, or viral. Unfortunately, these weapons and their ammo are quite heavy and using them can be exhausting. Thus they tend to remain a squad support weapon rather than standard equipment.

Unlike many other soldiers in the field, zombie hunters always carry a pistol. Zombie fights often occur at close quarters where pistols are easier to use. Also large zombie hordes can often overrun a position, leaving no time to reload a primary weapon. Again, every man is free to choose his own backup weapon, but they generally fall into one of two categories. Some hunters prefer a light pistol with low recoil and a big magazine, which is good for calmly making head shots against atomic and viral zombies. Others, generally older hunters, like something with more punch, like the Colt M1911. These are good for blasting apart necromantic zombies and are less likely to glance off thick zombie skulls. Either can be an effective tool in the hands of a trained professional.

Artwork by Marc Lee

HAND WEAPONS

Most zombie hunters carry a knife, but this is only a tool and not really a weapon. In point of fact, there are no hand weapons that can be said to be very effective against most types of zombie. When desperate, hunters look for a heavy-hitting, balanced weapon that is unlikely to get stuck in a zombie. Baseball bats and machetes make good choices, but neither is likely to survive for more than a couple of kills before breaking or bending. While it is true that broadswords and *katanas* are probably the best anti-zombie hand weapons, neither is in common manufacture and nor are they easy to carry.

HEAVY WEAPONS

The military learned early on in the zombie wars not to rely on explosive weapons against the undead. Immune to shock, concussion, shrapnel, and even losing limbs, only a direct hit from explosive devices is likely to take out most zombies. Instead, the best heavy weapon to use against zombies remains the good old-fashioned machine gun. While it is virtually impossible to make an aimed head shot with a Browning .50, it hardly matters when the heavy slugs literally tear the target zombie to pieces. Other members of the team can pick off the ones that are still crawling after the hail of bullets. The most devastating anti-zombie weapon is probably the minigun (a vehicle-mounted machine gun with rotating barrels), which is often carried by the helicopter support for containment teams.

Having abandoned most sorts of grenade except signal smoke, most government hunter teams carry some form of directional anti-personnel scatterfire mine such as a claymore. These weapons work much like giant shotguns or canister shot in Napoleonic cannons, firing hundreds of ball-bearings in one direction. Any time a hunter team decides to hold a fixed position, one of their first tasks is to set up claymores. Triggering a couple of claymores against a close-packed horde can have devastating effects.

ARMOR

The rising zombie threat forced military authorities to completely rethink personal body armor. Bulletproof vests and flak jackets were both unnecessarily bulky and provided little protection to areas mostly like to receive zombie wounds. Today, zombie hunters wear loose-fitting body suits made of a variety of extremely strong fabrics. They are virtually impossible to tear with bare hands, and most zombies will have

REAPER 1 AND REAPER 2

During the 1988 Cerro Gordo, Iowa outbreak, local landscaper Neil Bower used a John Deere combine harvester to single-handedly eliminate a 300-strong zombie horde. The incident did not go unnoticed by the US government. Three years later, the military began field testing *Reaper 1*, a purpose-built zombie harvester. Initial trials found that the blades had a tendency to gum up after the first few dozen zombies, and the designers had greatly underestimated the "splatter effect," which sent potentially deadly zombie-infected matter in all directions.

By 1996, the military had created *Reaper 2* as the ultimate zombie-fighting weapon, incorporating the lessons learned from *Reaper 1*. Smaller than a full-sized combine harvester, *Reaper 2* still towers twelve feet above the ground. It has a cockpit team of two, a driver and the commander who also rides shotgun, picking off any zombies that manage to survive the blades and cling onto the side. The vehicle can also carry six passengers and stocks a full communications array. The designers created *Reaper 2* so that it could be disassembled into eight component parts, allowing it to be airlifted to trouble spots. While the deployment of *Reaper 2* remains highly classified, there is evidence that it has been used on at least five different occasions in the last fifteen years.

US Army

Black Hawk helicopters have proved very effective in the military's fight against zombies.

to chew for a while to get to the human underneath. While providing excellent protection, they hardly render someone immune to zombie attacks. It is not necessary to get through the clothes to mangle the human inside, and zombies are nothing if not determined when it comes to killing, eating, or infecting.

Along with the suit, hunters generally wear a selection of commercially available sporting protection. Hockey helmets remain popular, as do elbow and knee pads. It is easy to shatter your own elbow smashing it into a zombie skull.

NUCLEAR, CHEMICAL, AND BIOLOGICAL GEAR

Some of the first NATO containment teams went into action wearing full Nuclear, Biological, and Chemical (NBC) suits, but this was quickly deemed unnecessary in most situations. These days, full suits are generally only worn by the clean-up crews that come in after the frontline containment teams to finish off any stragglers and dispose of infected bodies.

Standard soldiers do carry some defense against these elements. All hunters carry Geiger counters, both to warn them of a dangerous environment, but also to detect the possibility of rad zombies. Also, no zombie hunter is sent into combat without a couple of syringes full of anti-viral solution strapped into a high-impact container. Finally, zombie hunters are always equipped with a gas mask. This piece of equipment remains vital when dealing with viral zombies. It is easy to become infected even without getting wounded when fighting at close quarters. Any blood or tissue splattered into the mouth or even eyes can lead to infection. Most hunters will not go into combat wearing a mask, but will keep it close at hand for the minute that a situation turns dicey.

VEHICLES

Vehicles remain a double-edged sword in the war against zombies. Without them, it would be impossible to mount the quick response necessary to contain outbreaks. They are also valuable as mobile gun platforms, means of evacuation, and offensive strike weapons. On the other hand, the noise generated by even the quietest vehicles makes them zombie magnets, and driving into an outbreak area will quickly generate a horde.

Probably the most important vehicle in the zombie wars is the helicopter. Almost all containment teams are airborne trained, and helicopter deployment remains their number-one means of reaching a target zone. Helicopters can also remain on station to provide fire support and aerial reconnaissance. Unfortunately, unlike ground vehicles, it is never possible to turn off the engine and sit quietly if necessary.

Larger military vehicles such as tanks and armored personnel carriers are rarely employed against the undead. While their sheer bulk makes them capable zombie squashers, most governments have found them inefficient and difficult to transport. Most containment teams use modified versions of their military's main utility vehicle, such as the Humvee, sporting extra armor over the windshield and windows, and often employing a ram or cowcatcher on the front.

Zombie Hunter Tactics

"An outbreak of zombies infecting humans is likely to be disastrous, unless extremely aggressive tactics are employed against the undead."
When Zombies Attack!: Mathematical Modelling of an Outbreak of Zombie Infection by Philip Munz, Ioan Hudea, Joe Imad, and Robert J. Smith

Any discussion of tactics is fraught with peril. Rarely does any military operation, zombie or conventional, run strictly by the book. Every situation is unique and to try to impose a rigid adherence to one set of practices can only lead to disaster. While this chapter presents a brief overview of how most zombie hunter organizations attempt to run a modern containment operation, it is doubtful if any operation has ever run as smoothly as the idea presented here. Also, this presentation only applies to countries that have specialized containment teams on call.

In the event of a reported outbreak, a single zombie hunter element (usually one squad or fire team) is airlifted via helicopter to the area. If the outbreak is in a town or city, the helicopter touches down just outside the urban area, and the hunters deploy. After the helicopter again lifts off, it circles around the target area to run reconnaissance. Meanwhile the hunters advance on foot. Nine times out of ten, the incident turns out to be a false alarm and the whole maneuver is written off as a drill. However, if either the team or the helicopter spots evidence of zombie infestation, they will immediately radio back to base to prepare for a full-scale containment.

The original hunter team remains on site to gather further information, most importantly determining the variety of zombie threat. In the case of a revenant, the team will immediately go on the offensive, trying to keep the revenant occupied until reinforcements arrive. If the zombies appear to be necromantic, including voodoo, the hunters attempt to remain concealed while searching for the necromancer behind the disturbance. If the outbreak proves to be either atomic or viral, the team will launch limited offensive operations. It is always easiest to stop a viral or atomic outbreak just as it is beginning, and if the team can take out any zombies early, they may save countless lives and prevent untold numbers of zombies being created later. Of course, when human lives are at stake, zombie hunters often get caught up in events on the ground and the theories are left behind by the practicalities of survival.

Once alerted to an actual threat, a full containment team will be launched. In the United States, this would mean the entire 34th Specialist Regiment. A full mobilization usually takes one to two days, depending on the remoteness of the outbreak area. During this time, the target area is surrounded by the containment team. Usually, a dozen separate bases or checkpoints are established along the major roads or at access points to the area. From these positions, constant patrols are sent in all directions to ensure no zombies are slipping through the net to infect other areas. The men on the ground are supported by helicopters and, in some cases, unmanned drones.

Room clearance

The attached diagram depicts the standard tactical practice of a US Army containment team engaged in clearing a room of any possible zombie threat. While the particulars are specific to US Army doctrine, most governments which employ containment teams use similar techniques.

Trooper A is the squad heavy. In most cases, he will be equipped with the AA-12 automatic shotgun. Trooper A stands several paces in front of the rest of the team. He will take no part in the actual room assault unless commanded to do so by the team leader. His job is to guard against potential threats from deeper within the building. In the case of individual zombies advancing on his position, he is expected to carefully neutralize the threat. Should a zombie horde appear, he must alert the rest of the team, while using his heavy firepower to hold the horde back long enough for the team to begin extraction.

Trooper B is the team leader. He stands several paces to the rear and is armed with the standard M4A1 carbine. His task is to provide rear security and maintain a grasp of the overall situation. While his task is similar to Trooper A, a careful building clearance should reduce the threat of attack from behind.

Trooper C stands directly in front of the door of the target room. At this point, he will sling his carbine and draw his sidearm. The specific sidearm will vary from trooper to trooper. Trooper C's first task is to open the door. As soon as the door is open, Trooper C takes one step into the room (**Point 1**) and turns to face the near corner opposite to the direction the door opened (The near right corner in this case). Eliminating any potential threats in this corner

Trooper C must immediately advance several paces toward the far corner on the same side of the room (**Point 2**) so as to make space for Trooper D.

Trooper D begins the assault next to Trooper C, standing on the side opposite to the door hinges. As soon as Trooper C advances out of the doorway toward one far corner, Trooper D moves several paces toward the other far corner. Trooper D's first task is to make sure that no zombies are concealed behind the door. Although the door itself provides a momentary shield for Trooper C, the location behind the door is the most dangerous in the room, as any zombie located there will also be protected. Once any threat behind the door has been neutralized, Trooper D must turn his attention to the far corner on his side of the room. It is hoped that by this point, Trooper C will also be able to focus on this area.

A key note to this diagram: Troopers C and D only advance into the room as far as is necessary to move freely and to see all corners of the room. Distance from the zombie threat remains vital, even in the narrow confines of room clearance. Once the room has been fully checked and all zombies have been eliminated, Troopers C and D rejoin the rest of their team outside the room and the process is repeated in the next room. Room clearance is a painstakingly slow, but absolutely necessary part of any zombie containment.

Key:

Trooper

Zombie

Dead zombie

B
C
D
A
1
2
3

Artwork by Charlie Adlard

As the containment is being established, a number of sorties are launched into the outbreak area with the purpose of bringing out survivors. Most of these sorties are conducted by individual fire teams on foot, though they remain in constant contact with ground and air transport, as either will be made available for emergency evacuation. These teams advance as far as they can into the zone, rounding up the living and escorting them back to the containment line. At all costs, the teams must avoid alerting and causing the movement of a horde toward the lines.

By the time the containment lines are fully established, the variety of zombie threat should have been determined. In the case of necromantics, the containment team will immediately go on the offensive, launching a massive attack from one side of the circle and attempting to overwhelm the horde with superior firepower. While the main attack goes straight after the zombies, a number of small teams attempt to infiltrate behind the lines in search of the necromancer. Most of the time the necromancer cannot be located and the mission becomes one messy clean-up operation.

If it is determined that the zombies are either viral or atomic, a completely different strategy is employed. Instead of going on the offensive, the containment team selects a portion of its line and reinforces it with field fortifications, claymores, and emplaced weapons, setting up a defense in depth. Once this is done, a vehicle-mounted attack element is sent into the outbreak area with the specific intent of causing a zombie horde to advance toward the fortified section of the line. By baiting the zombie horde, it can be coaxed into a kill zone and wiped out by overwhelming firepower. Once the containment team destroys the main horde, it goes on the offensive, slowly collapsing the containment circle, eliminating all zombies encountered.

Artwork by Ben Rollman

Most containment teams, such as the 34th, are organized to independently cope with an outbreak in a small town or village. Should the outbreak take place in a major city, or spread throughout a whole region, obviously further military aid would be needed. In this case, the general military provides the manpower to form the containment lines, while the specialist zombie hunters run sorties and handle most of the direct combat.

To date, the battle of Mexico City remains the single largest recorded zombie outbreak since the American Civil War. This battle saw the employment of tactics similar to those described above. However, if the infection had managed to spread beyond the confines of the city, or if the number of infected had reached hundreds of thousands instead of just thousands, it is likely that such tactics would not have been effective. It remains imperative that all zombie outbreaks are contained as swiftly as possible. If the governments of the world have a plan or strategy in the event of a cataclysmic outbreak, it remains tightly under wraps. It is clear, however, that such an event would force some difficult moral decisions, that some would have to be sacrificed to save the whole. Let us pray that it never comes to that.

Further Reading, Watching, and Gaming

The following list includes many of my favorite zombie-related items. It is far from exhaustive, but should give anyone a good start on their own delving into the world of the zombie.

BOOKS

The Serpent and the Rainbow* & *The Passage of Darkness: The Ethnobiology of the Haitian Zombie by Wade Davis. The premiere books about "real" zombies in Haiti.

The Zombie Survival Guide by Max Brooks. The book that launched the current zombie publishing boom.

World War Z by Max Brooks. A global history of a zombie "doomsday" scenario, and arguably the best zombie book ever written.

Day by Day Armageddon by J. L. Bourne. My personal favorite first-person zombie survival story.

COMIC BOOKS

The Walking Dead by Robert Kirkman, Tony Moore, and Charlie Adlard. Having already run for over seventy issues, this ongoing drama has established itself as the most successful zombie comic book to date. Thanks to the generosity of Charlie Adlard and Robert Kirkman, several pieces of artwork from this series have been reprinted in this book.

GAMES

Artwork by Amanda Spaid

Zombies!!! by Twilight Creations. Containing over 100 plastic zombies, this delightful little board game plays more like a video game.

Last Night on Earth, The Zombie Game by Flying Frog Productions. Another good board game where participants can play either survivors or zombies. The game also comes with its own soundtrack!

Ambush Z by Ambush Alley Games. A terrific wargame, focusing on military actions against the zombie threat. Probably the best game for recreating the actions of professional containment teams.

Undead States of America. Another great wargame designed to refight zombie battles on an epic scale.

All Things Zombie by Two Hour Wargames. Perhaps the most popular wargame rules for outbreak survivor vs. zombie confrontations.

MOVIES

The White Zombie (1932). The first feature-length zombie film, starring Béla Lugosi.

Night of the Living Dead (1968). A small-budget, independent movie directed by George Romero, it truly launched the zombie film genre and remains one of its strongest examples.

Dawn of the Dead (1978). Romero's unconnected follow-up to *Night of the Living Dead* cemented his reputation as the greatest zombie director of all time.

28 Days Later (2002). Revitalized the zombie genre for a new generation and brought the idea of fast-virus zombies into the mainstream.

Shaun of the Dead (2004). Both a hilarious spoof and a good zombie movie at the same time, the movie helped open the zombie genre to a wider audience.

Glossary

Aggressor zombies	A variety of viral zombie that is faster and more aggressive than the normal viral zombie.
Atomic zombies	Zombies created through a chemical or radioactive contamination of a specific geographic area.
The Brotherhood of Death	An organization founded by Adolf Hitler after the dissolution of the Society of Thule; it included all of the foremost occultists from the old society.
Bureau 9	An organization founded by Allan Pinkerton during the American Civil War to combat the zombie threat. It continues to function in that capacity even today.
The "Cloak Room"	A secret suite of rooms hidden beneath the British World War II codebreaking center at Bletchley Park. It served as the Headquarters for Supreme Allied Command: Shadow Theater (SAC:ST).
Command: The Blue Marble (C:TBM)	An organization of mercenary soldiers trained as zombie hunters.
Containment Teams	Specialist multinational teams within the military forces of NATO countries that can deploy quickly to suppress zombie outbreaks.
Division 77, "The Dirge"	Zombie-containment team of the British military.
Draugr	Walking corpses from Norse/Viking mythology.
Grimoire	A book of spells or a manual for the use of black magic.
The Honourable Society of the Resurrection Men	A group founded in 1756 in Edinburgh by an unknown group of body-snatchers to fight the influx of necromancers in the city.
Horde	Any gathering of at least ten zombies where they are grouped closely enough that each member can hear the moans of at least three other members.
Irradiated zombies or "rad zombies"	The walking dead that have been exposed to dangerous levels of radiation and now carry that radiation inside their lifeless shell.
Liche	An undead necromancer.
The "Moan"	A dry, warbling sound produced by some varieties of zombies that appears to be a primitive means of communication among them.

Necromancer	One who uses necromancy or the magic of death.
Necromancy	Black magic; the practice of using the dead in magical rituals.
Necromantic zombies	Zombies created using black magic to reanimate the bodies of the dead.
"Nightmen"	Nickname of the members of the US Army 34th Specialist Regiment, which specializes in zombie containment.
Operation *Eklipse*	A World War II German mission to find certain religious artifacts, with the aim of using them to facilitate the creation of zombies in far larger numbers.
Reaper 1* and *Reaper 2	Harvester-type vehicles created to combat large groups of zombies efficiently.
Revenants	A variety of zombie reawakened by a force that seems to come completely from within the deceased individual.
Society of Thule	A secret order founded in Munich, Germany, by a World War I veteran, devoted to the pursuit of necromantic knowledge.
Supreme Allied Command: Shadow Theater (SAC:ST)	A secret Allied organization formed during World War II to combat the threat of the Nazi occult program.
Todesritter	"Death Knights" – a unit of zombie soldiers unleashed by Hitler during World War II.
Viral hounds	Zombie canines.
Viral zombies	Zombies created through a contagious virus that infects the living and turns them into zombies, following the rapid onset of death.
Voodoo	A magical and religious practice, often involving witchcraft and necromancy, largely centered in the islands of the Caribbean Sea
Voodoo zombie	A particular form of necromantic zombie created through the use of voodoo.
Z-virus	The virus that creates zombies.
The Zombie Dueling Association	An underground gladiatorial society which pits captured zombies against hired gladiators.
Zombie hunters	Those who hunt down and try to eliminate the threat represented by zombies.
Zombie master	A term once applied to necromancers who had assembled a large force of zombie minions, but has recently become more commonly associated with a zombie Typhoid Mary: a living human who carries the zombie virus and can transmit it to others without suffering its effects.

Index

Figures in **bold** refer to illustrations.